PENGUIN BOOKS
THE FUTURE OF INDIA

Bimal Jalan is one of India's well-known economists. He was Governor of the Reserve Bank of India from 1997 to 2003, demitting office on his nomination to the Upper House of Parliament by the President for distinguished service to the country. He has held several top positions in the ministries of finance and industry and in the Planning Commission. He was also Chairman of the Economic Advisory Council to the Prime Minister and represented India on the boards of the IMF and the World Bank.

He was educated at Presidency College, Calcutta, and Cambridge and Oxford universities. His books include *India's Economic Crisis: The Way Ahead* (1991), *India's Economic Policy: Preparing for the Twenty-first Century* (1996), *India's Economy in the New Millennium* (2002) and, as editor, *The Indian Economy: Problems and Prospects* (Revised edition, 2004).

The Future of India

Politics, Economics and Governance

BIMAL JALAN

PENGUIN BOOKS

PENGUIN BOOKS
Published by the Penguin Group
Penguin Books India Pvt. Ltd, 11 Community Centre, Panchsheel Park,
New Delhi 110 017, India
Penguin Group (USA) Inc., 375 Hudson Street, New York, New York 10014, USA
Penguin Group (Canada), 90 Eglinton Avenue East, Suite 700, Toronto, Ontario,
M4P 2Y3, Canada (a division of Pearson Penguin Canada Inc.)
Penguin Books Ltd, 80 Strand, London WC2R 0RL, England
Penguin Ireland, 25 St Stephen's Green, Dublin 2, Ireland (a division of Penguin
Books Ltd)
Penguin Group (Australia), 250 Camberwell Road, Camberwell, Victoria 3124,
Australia (a division of Pearson Australia Group Pty Ltd)
Penguin Group (NZ), cnr Airborne and Rosedale Roads, Albany, Auckland 1310,
New Zealand (a division of Pearson New Zealand Ltd)
Penguin Group (South Africa) (Pty) Ltd, 24 Sturdee Avenue, Rosebank,
Johannesburg 2196, South Africa

Penguin Books Ltd, Registered Offices: 80 Strand, London WC2R 0RL, England

First published in Viking by Penguin Books India 2005
Published in Penguin Books 2006

Copyright © Bimal Jalan 2005, 2006

10 9 8 7 6 5 4 3 2 1

ISBN-10: 0143062123; ISBN-13: 9780143062127

Typeset in Sabon Roman by SÜRYA, New Delhi
Printed at Anubha Printers, Noida

To
Maahira and Ayushman,
children of the twenty-first century,
and their future

Look back, therefore, as far as you can, drink deep of the eternal fountains that are behind, and after that, look forward, march forward and make India brighter, greater, much higher than she ever was.

—Swami Vivekananda

The achievement we celebrate today is but a step, an opening of opportunity, to the greater triumphs and achievements that await us. Are we brave enough and wise enough to grasp this opportunity and accept the challenge of the future?

—Jawaharlal Nehru, speech on the granting of independence.

Contents

Preface to the Second Edition

A new edition of a book provides a good opportunity to consider whether observations and assertions made in the previous edition require amendments in the light of reviews and other developments. After reflection, I believe that although the economic and political picture remains broadly the same as before, there is one vital difference. This is that the disjuncture between politics and economics that I had referred to (in Chapter II) has now become even more pronounced.

The economy is certainly more resilient and vibrant than was the case even a year ago. Growth rate is higher, inflation is lower, the external sector continues to be strong and the Sensex, the stock market index, is at an all-time high. There has been blossoming of Indian entrepreneurship. The Indian corporate sector is more confident now than ever before. The international accolade for India's economic future is louder, and there is a strong belief that India and China will be the dominant economies of the twenty-first century.

Domestic politics, on the other hand, has become more fluid and uncertain, particularly in the states. In several states, different combination of parties with widely divergent ideology and programmes have formed pre- or post-electoral alliances to acquire power. Fortunately for India, the Union government at the Centre has been stable under the leadership of a distinguished person who is universally admired for his integrity and high intellect. Despite internal differences as well as frequent disruptions, the Parliament has also unanimously passed several bills of historic importance, such as the Right to Information Bill, Women's Succession Bill, and Rural Employment Guarantee Bill. At the same time, hardly a week passes by when a fresh and bitter political controversy on a domestic or an external issue does not arise. This has made the efficient governance of the country difficult. It is also doubtful whether the government would have been able to survive in the face of several unsavoury episodes involving Cabinet ministers and dignitaries and judicial strictures (for example, in respect of dissolution of Bihar assembly in 2005)—but for the high personal credibility of its leader.

As politics has become curiouser and the economy has become more vibrant, a view is emerging—particularly among the better-off sections—that politics does not really matter all that much in determining economic outcomes. A central thesis of this book, on the other hand, is that effective governance and responsible politics are of utmost importance in shaping India's economic future. Is this conclusion still valid?

I strongly believe so. The crucial point that we must remember is that, after two or three years of high growth, exuberance about India's long-term economic future is not new. As highlighted in *The Future of India*, over the last fifty years, there have been at least three similar periods when the growth rate was as high as now, and everything looked very rosy. However, soon thereafter, the economy was plunged into prolonged periods of low growth and/or crises. It will also be recalled that, as recently as May 2004, when the earlier government was unexpectedly voted out of power, there was a sudden collapse of confidence, leading to a sharp decline in stock markets, because of political uncertainty. It will be premature to ignore the political role of the government in shaping the economic environment for growth with equity over the long run.

It is a sobering thought that, despite several favourable developments in the economy in the last decade, India continues to have the largest number of poor in the world, one of the lowest ranks in the global human development index, and a high degree of environmental pollution and deforestation. Public infrastructure, particularly in the rural areas, where the bulk of the people live, is by all accounts abysmal. The trend rate of growth of agriculture, which provides livelihood to 60 per cent of our population, has also been well below expectations. The share of India's agriculture in national income is now only about 20 per cent. The organized sector of the economy has grown, but employment has not increased.

Can all these negative features of India's socio-economic landscape be changed without strong government action, an efficient public delivery system and a responsive political environment? Over the long run, say ten or twenty years from now, can certain segments of the economy which benefit a minority of India's population, and some urban conglomerations, continue to grow at a high rate without purposive governmental action and political accountability for performance to the people at large (rather than to a handful of political leaders)? I have no doubt that the answer to both the questions has to be in the negative. If anything, the need for reform of the governance structure, the need to reduce the supply and demand of corruption, and the need to improve the functioning of our Parliamentary system are even more pressing now than before.

Except for correction of a couple of factual errors and redraft of a few sentences in the interest of greater clarity, the rest of the text in this edition is the same as the Viking edition published last year. The discussion by many experts and opinion-makers in public fora and the views expressed in journals and media reviews have been extremely helpful. I am grateful to all those who have participated in this debate.

21 February 2006   Bimal Jalan

Preface to the First Edition

The Future of India: Politics, Economics and Governance is different in tone and content from my previous books. My earlier books dealt primarily, though not exclusively, with economic policy issues. There was a recognition of the political process and its impact on the evolution of economic policy over time. However, the primary focus was on economics. This book is much broader in content. It attempts to give equal, if not more, weight to politics and governance aspects in addition to economics, in determining the shape of India's economic policy and its social fabric. It is the interplay of these three forces—politics, economics and governance—which will jointly determine the future of India.

In my earlier books, while personal reflection could not be avoided altogether, to a large extent I had tried to be as analytical and 'objective' as possible. This book is much more introspective, with a fair degree of personal reflection and impressions. On issues of public importance, I have taken the liberty of saying what I believe even though on several of them the historical evidence may be mixed or the theoretical basis may be inconclusive.

Fortunately, there is now considerable interest among specialists and observers belonging to different disciplines in

Indian economic, social and political developments. The idea of writing this book evolved gradually as a result of reading the books of a number of eminent writers— economists, political scientists and philosophers—on a variety of subjects, including India's past and its future. A striking feature of most of the recent writings, cutting across different disciplines, is the universal admiration for India's democracy combined with dissatisfaction with its actual functioning and its failure to deliver sufficient benefits to the people. Another common theme is the recognition of its vast economic potential along with frustration with the slow pace of reforms in the governance and administrative structure. This book is an attempt to explore some of the issues that have been discussed in the recent literature on India from a somewhat different perspective—of someone who had the opportunity to observe at close quarters the interplay of economics, politics and governance in determining policy outcomes and their impact on the country's economy.

I should particularly acknowledge two recent books, among many others, which I found particularly useful, and which were influential in my further exploring the interconnection between politics and economics in the context of India. These are: *The Idea of India* by Sunil Khilnani (Penguin, London, 1998) and *The Future of Freedom* by Fareed Zakaria (Penguin-Viking, New Delhi, 2003). Both the books are exceedingly well written, perceptive and wide in scope. They cover a variety of issues about the working of democracies, including India (either specifically or as part of a wider discussion on worldwide trends of democratization and liberalism). They rightly refer to some of the emerging problems, for example, the abysmal failure of democratic laws and procedures to moderate the excessive powers exercised by the state and its ministers, and the growing influence of special interests in determining economic policy outcomes. However, their views on how to improve the system without destroying its benefits left me with mixed feelings. In particular, Zakaria's conclusion that what the world needs is 'not more democracy, but less' and that there is an inherent conflict between liberalism and democratization, in my view, raises more issues than it resolves.

On a personal note, I should clarify that my own professional work has been in the areas of economics and administration. I have had the privilege of working with several high-level political dignitaries and to observe the working of our political system at close quarters. However, I have no direct experience of party politics as a participant, or academic training in political science and theory. My observations on politics are largely those of a citizen-observer. I can only hope that this limitation will make the book of greater, and not less, interest to the average citizen who is involved in the working of our democracy and in determining its future.

I am grateful to K.D. Sharma for doing a splendid job of typing and putting together the manuscript for press. I am also thankful to G.C. Khulbe for his help. I owe a special debt of gratitude to David Davidar, an old friend and now Publisher of Penguin Canada; Thomas Abraham; and Krishan Chopra of Penguin India, who was painstaking in his efforts to improve the contents of the book. Without their encouragement and support at various stages, this book could not have been completed.

3 January 2005   Bimal Jalan

Introduction

Every ten or fifteen years since independence, India's reputation has swung from that of a land of great opportunity to that of a country with an uncertain future. At the beginning of the twenty-first century, India's reputation as a democracy and as an emerging global economic power is at its peak. On the other hand, not so long ago, in 1991, India went through one of its worst economic crises. With two short-lived central governments in two years prior to 1991, there was also a big question mark about the country's political future.

Similarly, in the 1950s, soon after independence, India was seen as the leader among developing countries and a strong voice, on their behalf, in international affairs. The position changed dramatically by the mid-1960s when, after a bad drought, India had to practically beg for food aid from the United States. This difficult period was followed by a triumphant return to power by the Congress government in the 1971 elections in the wake of a clarion call to 'Remove Poverty' (or *Garibi Hatao*) and support to Bangladesh in its struggle for independence. Just four years later, in 1975, a national Emergency was declared, followed by a restoration of democracy in 1977 which received worldwide attention. However, the new government, formed by a coalition of parties which were in opposition earlier, did not last long, and in 1979 the country was once again plunged into a deep economic crisis because of political uncertainty, sharp rise in oil prices and drought.

Taken as a whole, the period from 1966 to 1980 was effectively the darkest period for the Indian economy during the post-independence period. The annual growth rate was only about 3 per cent, population growth was higher than 2 per cent per annum (compared with the Plan target of 1.25 per cent), and annual growth in per capita income was less than 1 per cent. The pace of industrialization, which was expected to accelerate with higher investment and higher domestic savings, also plummeted. The rate of growth of industrial production during the period 1965 to 1980 was only 4 per cent per annum as compared with 7.7 per cent in the earlier fifteen years (1950 to 1965).

Against this dismal historical background, there has been a sea change in India's economic position in the last two decades of the twentieth century and the beginning of the twenty-first century. Despite the economic crisis of 1991, the average annual growth rate since 1981 has been close to 6 per cent, the per capita growth is about 4 per cent per annum, and average life expectancy is estimated to have improved from fifty in 1981 to sixty-five at the turn of the century. India is regarded as an emerging economic power, and is one of the fastest growing countries in the world. Only China has grown faster than India in the last twenty years. However, in view of recent management problems in public sector enterprises, particularly in the banking sector, there is increasing scepticism about the ability of the Chinese economy to maintain its growth momentum. India also has one of the highest levels of foreign exchange reserves in the world in relation to its external debt or share of international trade, and balance of payment problems are unlikely to occur again in the foreseeable future. In the light of these highly positive developments, it is now commonplace to project India as one of the three most important global economies by 2020 or 2025 (after United States and China). An annual growth rate of 7.5 to 8 per cent is expected to be within reach in the years ahead. In view of anticipated decline in population growth, per capita incomes may rise by 6 per cent or more per year. The increase in per capita income of this order would have a substantial impact in reducing poverty and eliminating hunger, malnutrition and illiteracy.

I too share the current optimism about India's capacity to grow faster than ever before and eliminate poverty within a reasonable period. At the same time, given the history of sharp swings in India's fortunes, there is also a nagging doubt whether there will in fact be a sufficient change in our political vision, economic policy and administrative system to seize the opportunities that lie ahead. This doubt has been reinforced by our inability to break through the 6 per cent growth barrier despite the post-1991 reforms, high foreign exchange reserves, excellence in information technology, and global capital mobility. The average growth rate climbed to about 6 per cent during the 1980s, but remained at about the same level during the 1990s.

This book is an attempt to understand the causes of the swings in India's fortunes from time to time, and explore the reasons for our failure to fully realize our potential. Ever since independence, India has been fortunate in having a string of highly reputed political leaders who did their best to lead the country under difficult circumstances. It has also had the advantage of having a large number of top economists of international stature to advise the government in the process of planning and economic policy formulation. In respect of administration, India inherited the so-called 'steel frame' of a permanent bureaucracy from the British era, which was the envy of the post-colonial developing world. And yet, despite all these advantages, over a period of nearly six decades after independence, economic progress has been much slower than anticipated or planned.

Looking at our record, my broad conclusion is that while on the surface economists, political leaders and administrators were working together, in a more fundamental sense the reality was vastly different. Despite appearances to the contrary, there was in fact a substantial gap between what was considered to be economically sound and what was found to be politically feasible. Economic strategy seldom reflected our political or social realities or real political considerations. Similarly, the administrative implications of policies, launched with great conviction, were seldom considered or, when considered, these implications did not affect the actual evolution of economic policies or programmes on the ground. For a better future and sustained high growth, it is essential to evolve policies that are practical and pragmatic, and can reconcile the country's economic interests with political realities within a democratic framework.

On the importance of keeping political factors in view while considering economic issues, I am reminded of Gunnar Myrdal's observation nearly fifty years ago when development economics and development planning were at an early stage. The only certainty, he reminded us, is that 'we shall continuously be surprised by seeing the unexpected happen'. Nothing is permanent, particularly political development.[1]

In considering economic policy issues from a political perspective, I believe that, as recently highlighted by I.M.D. Little (2003), it is necessary to make a conceptual distinction between the role of the 'State', and that of the 'Government' in power.[2] The State comprises all the legislative, executive and judicial institutions, and the laws governing the inhabitants of the territory to which it lays claim. It also has the monopoly of the use of force over its citizens and over foreigners (as only the State can declare war). Governments, on the other hand, may be thought of as being tenants of the State. They may come and go in accordance with the Constitution or customs of the State. While in office, a government in power—whether elected or unelected—may change the institutions and laws of the State, but at any given moment it is the agent of the State. While the State is expected to be permanent, the authority of the government to make policy is likely to last as long as it continues to be in office.

This conceptual distinction between State and Government, in my view, is vital as it explains why a government—even if freely and duly elected—has to be directly accountable to the people for its actions. The State is the sole and legitimate custodian of public interest and sovereign power, and not the government of the day. Public institutions are expected to be permanent (for example, say, the railways, or the universities), and they should not be allowed to be governed by the whims and fancies of the ministers 'temporarily' in power.

The Future of India is divided into five chapters, followed by an epilogue. The reader will notice that there is a strong emphasis on the political aspect in all the chapters, including the epilogue. The first and the fifth chapter deal exclusively with the evolution of democratic politics in our country, its strengths and weaknesses, and the changes that are required to make the political system work better for the benefit of the people as a whole, and not only in the interest of the leaders whom they elect. The second chapter deals with the process of economic policy making in the country, and the impact of colonial legacy and coalitions of special interests in keeping the pace of economic reforms slow and sub-optimal. The third and the fourth chapters are concerned with certain issues in the areas of governance and widespread corruption in our society, and suggest measures for reform. The epilogue is on 'a resurgent India'. It is a reflection on what needs to be done to revitalize India's institutions in order to realize the country's full potential and eliminate poverty once and for all. Although different aspects covering politics, economics and governance—and suggestions for dealing with some of the problems in these areas—are covered in separate chapters, I hope the reader will find the views expressed in them closely linked.

I have tried to make this introductory chapter as self-contained as possible so that a reader, if he or she so wishes, can get a reasonable account of the views contained in various chapters. I hope that the issues that have been highlighted, and the inter-connections among them, would lead to further work and debate among experts, subject specialists and policy makers on an appropriate agenda for the future.

Democracy, Politics and Economics

In May 2004, the country completed the general elections to the fourteenth Lok Sabha. In terms of the number of persons entitled to vote (about 675 million), and the number of persons who exercised their franchise (over 400 million), this was the largest democratic election ever held in the world. Indian elections are also, by and large, free and fair. All eligible voters irrespective of caste, creed, religion, income or occupation have equal rights. An autonomous Election Commission supervises the elections. It has the necessary powers to ensure that the right of voters to vote freely is respected in principle and in practice. The judiciary is vigilant and its verdict commands the full respect of all concerned, including the party and the government in power. For all Indians, and others interested in democratic elections, it is an exhilarating feeling to see all candidates, including powerful ministers and the prime minister, campaigning from time to time for people's votes with utmost humility and respect.

The elections are truly the hour of triumph for India's democratic traditions, which have set standards for other countries to follow. At the same time, as I reflect on what Indian democracy has been able to achieve for the people, apart from the right to vote, there is an unavoidable feeling of disappointment and unease. As soon as the elections are over, and a new government takes office (of whatever complexion and colour), the government becomes a power unto itself. The people's interests tend to be overtaken by the power of special interests and, in political scientist Mancur Olson's famous phrase, 'distributional coalitions'. These coalitions are generally more interested in influencing the distribution of wealth and income in their favour, rather than in the generation of additional output for the benefit of the public. Ministers and their bureaucrats become authoritarian, self-centred and autocratic. They are no doubt subject to some checks and balances by Parliament and the judiciary but, by and large, they are able to do as they wish. Their accountability to the public is also more apparent than real—at least until the next elections.

Thus, in the words of Pratap Bhanu Mehta (2003), a well-known writer on law and governance in India, 'the broad framework within which practices of popular authorization can be carried out remain intact, but politics itself has become an area where norms exist only in their breach . . . The very mechanism, designed to secure the liberty, well-being and dignity of citizens, representative democracy, is routinely throwing up forces that threaten to undermine it; the very laws that are supposed to enshrine republican aspirations are incapable of commanding minimal respect, and their inaction subjects the entire political process to ridicule. The corruption, mediocrity, indiscipline, venality and lack of moral imagination of the political class, those essential agents of representation in any democracy, makes them incapable of attending to the well-being of citizens' (p.17).[3]

The first chapter, 'The triumph and travails of democracy', examines the political forces involved in determining the evolution of economic policy in the country. Ian Little's distinction between the State and the government is crucial in explaining why the nationalist ideals of a State-directed development strategy as an essential component of political democracy did not achieve much. The powers of the State, enshrined in the Constitution, were exercised by the government in office. The government generally represented the interests of a political party (or a coalition of political parties). Political parties, in turn, represented the special interests of a section of the people rather than the country as a whole. In theory, under the Constitution, the responsibility for the policies and actions of the government and its cabinet was 'collective'. However, the prime minister or the chief minister had unfettered discretion in appointing his or her cabinet in consultation with a few top leaders of the party or parties in power. As a result, ministers, once appointed, enjoyed complete powers in respect of the business of their respective ministries as long as they enjoyed the confidence of the leader of their party.

A question which continues to puzzle most observers of

the Indian scene is: Why do the people of India, who have the right to vote freely and elect their own government, not exercise greater vigilance over the conduct of their elected representatives? Why do they continue to elect corrupt persons, several of them with criminal records, with narrow interests? In the 2004 elections, for example, it is difficult to understand why in large states like Bihar and Uttar Pradesh, which have such a decisive role in the formation of the government, a sizeable proportion of the electorate continues to support leaders and parties with an abysmal record of service to the people and little commitment to the growth and development of their respective states. The answer to these questions, in my view, really lies in the large incidence of illiteracy, particularly female illiteracy, in these states in particular and the country in general. In these states, according to available statistics, more than half the voters and nearly two-thirds of female voters are illiterate. As a result, local parties and political leaders are able to exploit caste, religious or regional factors to their own advantage. This underscores the importance of implementing the country's commitment to provide 'education for all' as a fundamental right. Literacy and education will not totally eliminate the importance of caste and religion in India, but it will certainly make the voters better informed and political parties more accountable.

India has a parliamentary system of government, and the government is expected to continue in office as long as it enjoys the confidence of the majority of the elected members in the Lok Sabha (House of the People). While in office, the government is accountable to both Houses of Parliament, the Lok Sabha and the Council of States (Rajya Sabha). The judiciary, with the Supreme Court at its apex, is independent of both government and Parliament, and its legal pronouncements are binding on all institutions of the

State and the public. It is also the custodian of the people's rights as well as the freedom of the press, as guaranteed in the Constitution.

This is the theory. In practice, the accountability of the government to Parliament and legislatures is perfunctory and minimal. The relevant rules of business, including regular question hours and calling attention motions, are duly in place and punctiliously observed by the government. However, as long as the government and the parties represented in it have the majority support in Parliament, they can literally get away with anything, including ministerial corruption and harassment of persons in opposition. Political parties, small and large, are firmly under the control of their leaders, and inner-party democracy is conspicuous by its absence from most parties. Therefore, by and large, the government is accountable only to a handful of leaders of the parties that are represented in the government. Ironically, in a coalition government, small local-party formations, with a pronounced loyalty to a particular caste or sect, can have a disproportionate influence in determining the course of government policies.

In practice, Parliament and legislatures generally do what the government wants them to do, rather than the other way round. Thus, for example, one of the most important functions of Parliament (which, in fact, was the primary reason for the American Revolution and the adoption of the Bill of Rights) is to approve the budget of the government and its taxation and expenditure proposals. In theory, the government cannot tax or spend without parliamentary or legislative authority. In practice, however, this authority is largely procedural. All expenditure and tax decisions are made by the minister of finance with the approval of the prime minister or chief minister, where necessary. The minister of finance would no doubt listen to the debate in Parliament and graciously amend some of the budgetary provisions, but, by and large, parliamentary approval is a mere formality.

The government's real accountability to the judiciary is also minimal. In interpreting the constitutional provisions relating to the legislative powers of the government or the division of powers between the centre and the states, judicial powers are supreme. The judiciary can determine the process through which a government decision has to be legitimized (for example, through parliamentary approval). Its judgements in respect of public interest petitions filed by citizens or the rights of individuals, particularly civil servants, are also binding. Nevertheless, a determined government can more or less do what it wants—except change the basic structure of the Constitution. It has unfettered powers to have new legislations passed as long as it has the majority, and except under very exceptional circumstances these statutory provisions are binding on the judiciary. So far as economic policies are concerned, the government's powers are virtually unlimited, provided appropriate business rules and legislative procedures have been followed.

The long delays in processing cases have further eroded the powers of the judiciary. Such delays are now legendary. No less than a former Chief Justice of the Supreme Court has given his legal opinion in a foreign court that India's judicial system is practically non-functional in settling commercial disputes. The non-functionality of the judicial system has been further compounded by the almost limitless powers of the government to notify 'rules' under Acts passed by Parliament or legislatures. The actual statutory provisions, as approved by Parliament, may provide for 'due process' and accountability. However, all Acts of Parliament generally have an omnibus provision whereby the government is free to make 'rules' under the relevant

Act through executive notifications. An example of this phenomenon is the government's right to make rules under the 'Freedom of Information Bill', first passed by Parliament in January 2003. The Bill did not come into force, despite the President having given his assent, as the government did not issue the necessary notification. The 2002 Bill was replaced by another Bill in December 2004. The new bill was again passed by the Parliament and finally notified in June 2005. This was two and a half years after this important bill was first approved. The amended Act is certainly better than the previous bill in scope and content. However, it also provides considerable discretion to the government to 'make rules' on any matter it considers appropriate.

As Amartya Sen has so eloquently argued in his writings and speeches, for the people of India, democracy is its own reward and the benefits of freedom cannot be judged solely in terms of its contribution to growth or economic well-being. In any case, recent empirical research has established that there is no direct association between success in growth or poverty alleviation and the form of government. Authoritarian governments are as prone to economic failure, if not more, as democracies. At the same time, as Sen has also observed, valuable as democracy is as a major source of social opportunity, there is a strong need to examine the ways and means of making it function well and realize its full potential. Eternal vigilance on the part of the people is indeed the price of liberty. There is no room for complacency on this score.

The second chapter, 'The economics of non-performance', deals with certain factors which may impede India's growth over the long run, despite the upsurge of interest and confidence in India's economy in recent years. At present, based on its performance, there is an emerging consensus that, *if India follows the right policies*, by 2020 or 2025, it would be the third largest economy in the world.

There is no doubt that the opportunities for India to accelerate its rate of growth further (to, say, 8 per cent or more) and eliminate poverty by improving the public delivery system are much better today than at any other time in the previous half-century. Part of the reason for this resurgence of confidence in India's future is no doubt the process of economic reforms initiated in 1991. However, there is also another important reason why there has been such a dramatic shift in India's economic outlook. The basic reason, which is sometimes overlooked, is that the sources of comparative advantage of nations are vastly different today than they were fifty or even twenty years ago. There are very few developing countries that are as well placed as India to take advantage of the phenomenal changes that have occurred in production technologies, international trade, capital movement and the deployment of skilled manpower. As a result, India today has the knowledge and the skills to produce and process a wide variety of products and services at competitive costs.

The opportunities for it to achieve a high growth rate and eliminate poverty in the foreseeable future are thus immense. All observers of the Indian economy, including governments in power, also generally agree that in order to realize its full potential in the new global environment, it is necessary for India to make a decisive move towards deeper reforms and reduce the pervasive procedural and administrative bottlenecks. While there is agreement in principle for a new policy orientation, looking at our record, I am not at all confident that we will be able to fully seize the opportunities that are now available. There are primarily three factors which are likely to impede India's progress. These are: the deadweight of the past, the power of distributional coalitions, and the growing disjuncture between economics and politics.

Even after more than half a century of development

experience, India's vision of the future continues to be clouded by beliefs which have failed to yield expected results in terms of growth, investment and savings. In view of the colonial experience of foreign domination, economic stagnation, and increasing poverty, the post-independence development strategy had given very high priority to making India economically independent. Based on the Soviet experience, it was believed that economic independence and high domestic savings could be achieved only if the 'commanding heights' of the economy were in the hands of the public sector, and dependence on foreign investment was reduced. It was assumed that if the means of production were owned by the State, all the value added in production would flow to the people. Further, if consumption was discouraged, public savings would automatically increase. These savings could then be used for further investment and growth, and India could soon catch up with the developed world. This was a most heart-warming economic vision, supported by leading economists of the day and widely respected academic models of savings, investment and growth.

However, it was soon evident that instead of generating savings, the public sector had become a drain on public savings. Despite its occupying the 'commanding heights', by the end of the 1990s, public sector savings were negative by as much as 4 per cent of GDP. These negative savings led to fast accumulation of internal public debt and lower investment than would have been the case otherwise. In the annals of development history, it is hard to find another example of a perfectly sensible idea—the need for higher public investment for greater public good—leading to exactly the opposite result: higher public consumption with diminishing returns for the public!

Why did such unrealistic assumptions about sources of

growth in public savings and investment persist for so long? Ever since independence, India was fortunate in having a string of top development economists and thinkers to advise the government in the process of planning and economic policy formulation—among them were well-known names like Prof. P.C. Mahalanobis, Dr Pitambar Pant and Prof. Raj Krishna. Yet, the results in terms of social or economic development—leaving aside the most recent period—were disappointing. Part of the reason for this sorry state of affairs was that economic and development strategy, propounded by the best economic brains and enshrined in successive Five Year Plans, seldom reflected the political and administrative realities on the ground. The political assumption underlying the favoured economic strategy was that the control over allocation of the country's savings by elected politicians would ensure that all such savings were used to promote the best interests of the country's poor in the most efficient manner. The administrative assumption was that the required bureaucratic response to implement the government's development programmes would be forthcoming in abundant measure. The system of administration at different levels was expected to work in complete harmony, delivering savings and investments as postulated in the development models and implementing government programmes as planned.

These political and administrative assumptions, unfortunately, turned out to be unrealistic. Nevertheless, as so often happens, theories once propounded and accepted as ideal are difficult to discard even if the results turn out to be different from what was expected. Various alibis for unsatisfactory outcomes are usually advanced to justify the initial choice of strategy accompanied by exhortations for better performance in the future. There is also a marked tendency among distinguished development theorists, both on the left and the right, to take ideological positions on such matters as planning and the appropriate role of the State in the economy irrespective of the country's institutional structure, its social realities and the global environment.

Looking back, it is amazing how much of the economic and political debate on future strategy is still conditioned by the colonial legacy. Irrespective of which party or coalition of parties is in power, political leaders (with very few exceptions) continue to express their confidence in the ability of the public sector to generate savings for further investment in the economy. Similarly, while availability of capital is no longer a constraint to development in view of international capital mobility, the same old mindset, based on the colonial experience, continues to dominate India's approach to foreign investment. At the beginning of the twenty-first century, unlike the situation fifty or a hundred years ago, the share of foreign direct investment is among the lowest in the world and relatively insignificant in relation to the size of the economy. India's industry and infrastructure are now largely owned by Indians. Yet, policies to liberalize foreign investment continue to attract considerable political controversy.

The hangover of the past is also reflected in the continuing dominant role of the bureaucracy in determining policy outcomes. It must be said to the credit of our planners that as early as 1956, the Second Plan did ask itself the question whether the civil service would prove equal to the tasks assigned to it by the Plan. The subsequent Plans also expressed their desperation about widespread administrative inefficiencies and bottlenecks that were slowing down the economy. However, this desperation was not reflected in the actual planning. We went on adding newer, larger and more comprehensive schemes to tackle national problems in virtually every walk of life, calling for greater and greater administrative involvement.

Thus, although there has been substantial policy liberalization in respect of corporate investments in the economy during the 1990s, the regulatory and administrative processes that are required for the various kinds of approvals (from land acquisition to environmental clearance) continue as before and, in some respects, have become worse. There are multiple government agencies in place, which work at cross purposes with each other. The number of permissions required to set up an industry and the number of inspectors involved in the bargaining process of granting such permissions have in fact increased over time. In the capital city of Delhi, for example, for land acquisition and associated permissions, as many as five agencies—each working at cross purposes with the other—are involved (the Urban Development Department, the New Delhi Municipal Committee, the Municipal Corporation of Delhi, the Delhi Development Authority and the Public Works Department).[4] In a crucial area such as public health, one ministry (the Ministry of Health) is responsible for ensuring the availability of good quality drugs in all parts of the country. However, it is a different ministry (the Ministry of Chemicals and Fertilizers) which is responsible for the production, regulation and distribution of drugs and medicines. The former ministry is in favour of encouraging units, irrespective of their size, to produce high-quality drugs by employing state-of-the-art technology. The latter ministry is in favour of promoting small-scale firms, irrespective of their ability to provide the necessary infrastructure for quality control![5]

The procedural complexity and administrative apathy are widely known and appreciated even at the higher levels of the government. However, it has not been feasible to bring about any systematic improvement because of the immense power of the coalition of special interests that benefited greatly from the old strategy of centralized control at the expense of the general public. Political leaders gained, and are still gaining, from their control over the resources of the public sector enterprises, their power to regulate the activities of large private sector enterprises, their power to fix prices of agricultural and industrial goods, and their ability to provide subsidies and incur fiscal deficits. Workers in the organized sector, in both the public and the private sectors, gained from the immense powers and political patronage enjoyed by them. Bureaucrats gained from opportunities for corruption at different levels of the administration, and statutorily guaranteed security for their jobs. Private sector entrepreneurs and contractors gained from their ability to influence government decisions in their favour through higher protection or preferential contracts, particularly during elections, which were taking place with increasing frequency.

These coalitions of special interests ensured that the necessary change in the initial development strategy did not occur for as long as possible, and when it became unavoidable (due to external crises), it was slow and politically controversial. I believe that an understanding of this experience is necessary so that its repetition can be avoided in the future. We must be willing and ready to change strategy and policies when initial conditions have changed. This can happen only if public policy, *ab initio*, guards against the emergence and entrenchment of special interests by limiting governmental and bureaucratic powers.

In this connection, a core issue with multiple dimensions, which would need to be resolved in the years to come, is what can perhaps be described as the growing 'public–private' dichotomy in our economic life. It is a striking fact that economic renewal and positive growth impulses are now occurring largely outside the public sector—at the levels of private corporations, autonomous institutions and individuals at the top of their professions in India and abroad. In the governmental or public sector, on the other hand, we see a marked deterioration at all levels—not only in terms of output, profits and public savings, but also in the provision of vital public services in the fields of education, health, water and transport. These two elements—fiscal deterioration and the inability to provide essential services—are, of course, intimately connected. Most of our public resources are dissipated in the payment of salaries or interest on debt, with little or no resources available for the expansion of public or publicly supported services in vital sectors.

Another phenomenon which is likely to impede economic progress is the growing disjuncture between economics and politics in India. It is increasingly evident that despite the spread of political democracy to all parts of India, which is a laudable achievement, a government's performance in regard to the growth rate or alleviation of poverty is not an important factor in determining electoral outcomes. Thus, in recent years, governments which have performed relatively well economically have lost elections at the centre (for example, the Congress government in 1996 or the coalition led by the Bharatiya Janata Party in 2004). Similarly, states which have performed very poorly in economic terms or in implementing anti-poverty programmes continue to return parties to power which are responsible for this state of affairs.

Taking these factors into account, my broad conclusion is that it cannot yet be taken for granted that India will be able to achieve its full economic potential or succeed in substantially accelerating its growth rate beyond what was achieved in the 1990s or even the 1980s. I hope that the real outcome will be better than what past trends indicate and that there will be a change in the power of dominant coalitions and the old mindset in determining India's economic strategy.

Governance and Corruption

At independence, India inherited a colonial State and kept much of its governance structure intact. By all accounts, during the colonial period, the administrative structure devised by the British was efficient in meeting its limited objectives. It was highly authoritarian and remote so far as the general public was concerned. Its primary purpose was to maintain law and order, and promote Britain's trading interests as per the laws enacted by the British. The same governance architecture was asked to bear the full load of centralized planning and a multitude of public programmes after independence. With rising expectations and the failure to deliver what was promised in the second and subsequent Plans, newer and more comprehensive government schemes were introduced in virtually every walk of life. These posed new administrative challenges in an environment of diminishing fiscal resources, periodic external crises and mounting procedural complexities.

As the administrative system became less efficient and more complex, requiring more and more public servants to perform the same tasks, it acquired a momentum of its own. With rising wages, periodic Pay Commissions, and judicial pronouncements in favour of government employees, the so-called public servants soon became their own masters, with little accountability to the people or their representatives. As government service became the most attractive source of employment, the vested interests of politicians and power brokers ensured that more and more schemes and public programmes were added to the existing ones. Over time, the creation of government jobs became an end in itself, and administrative salaries and pensions became the main component of most schemes.

There is no doubt that India is now facing a crisis of governance. By any criterion, the administrative system is now largely non-functional and unresponsive to the economic and social priorities of the country. An important challenge for the future is to reform this system. This is by no means easy. A number of administrative reform commissions, committees and task forces have made numerous recommendations which have remained largely unimplemented because of the coalition of interests against reducing the number of government agencies, offices, jobs and privileges. Simplification of procedures, reduction of administrative layers and documentation have the effect of reducing the requirement of personnel and departments. As a result, there is no real incentive, or dominant interest, to make life easier for the people or improve the public delivery system.

Among other aspects, the chapter 'Crisis of governance' also examines the role of the civil service and that of the ministers in the administrative structure and the public delivery system. Both are essential pillars of this structure, but a redefinition of their relative roles—and the interrelationship with each other—is now necessary. The civil service suffers from a myriad of problems, which have accumulated over a number of decades. While job security is still very much present at all levels, the sense of financial security has changed at different levels of various services. The top levels, while low in number, feel less secure than before in view of the widening gap between monetary compensation in civil services and the private sector. The lower rungs of the service, which account for the vast majority of the employees, enjoy compensation which is twice as high as equivalent levels in the private organized sector. Higher level jobs are transferable across the country as well as between departments, while lower level jobs are non-transferable. Tenures have become shorter for transferable jobs, while access to various requirements, such as housing or education, have become more difficult. The combined effect of all these pulls and pressures is that government and public sector jobs have become progressively less attractive at the top but immensely more attractive at clerical levels because alternative employment opportunities, partly as a result of antiquated labour laws, have shrunk.

Over the last five decades, there have also been significant changes in the role of ministers in the governance of the country. With the expansion of schemes, programmes, laws and rules in an environment of fiscal stringency, the number of ministries and ministers involved in actual decision making has increased substantially. Within the same ministry, several departments are likely to be involved in the formulation of policies and implementation of programmes. With multiple agencies and departments, generally working at cross purposes, the differences in views and policy approaches have to be resolved at higher and higher levels. This has resulted in the formation of a number of permanent or ad hoc cabinet committees and groups of ministers, which meet from time to time and from case to case. Alongside, with several parties in power in the states and at the centre, the tenures of ministers have also generally become shorter than they were when only one political party was in power at the centre as well as in most of the states. The expectation of a short tenure in government has had a profound impact on the relationship between ministers and civil servants. Each new party in power is keen to exercise its powers of transfers and postings to serve its interests. Accountability for performance in the implementation of programmes and policies has also become minimal as most ministers do not expect to be in power for very long.

The decay in the country's administrative and public delivery systems has affected the poor the most. They are critically dependent on the availability of public services and essential infrastructure, particularly in rural areas where 700 million or more of the people live. A redefinition of the powers and the role of ministers and civil servants in decision-making processes, and their accountability for performance are essential if India is to succeed in eliminating the worst forms of poverty in the midst of plenty.

At the ministerial level, a new institutional and constitutional initiative is required to hold individual ministers accountable for efficient delivery of public services and anti-poverty programmes. At present, ministers (such as those for rural development, water resources, health and anti-poverty programmes) are quick to announce ambitious annual or five-year targets for the benefit of the poor. However, no minister has actually been held accountable (or censured) for poor performance. The reason for non-accountability of individual ministers is the cherished doctrine of 'collective responsibility' of the council of ministers in a parliamentary form of government. In theory, the notion is that the government as a whole must resign if it loses the confidence of Parliament, and not only the erring minister. This hallowed doctrine, which evolved in the nineteenth century in Britain, has lost much of its relevance in India in view of the vast expansion of government activity in economic areas and increase in the power of individual ministers. The government is not only in charge of laying down the broad contours of macroeconomic policies, but also for implementing a whole host of projects and programmes at the micro level. Individual ministers can take virtually all decisions affecting public enterprises or projects under their charge, but they cannot be held accountable for the outcome. The impact of their decisions on project performance or public welfare is not a relevant consideration as long as the party to which they belong has a majority in Parliament. The non-accountability of ministers is particularly noticeable in coalition governments of disparate parties with a thin majority in Parliament or legislatures. Under these circumstances, the leader of even a small party, with less than 5 per cent of votes in Parliament, can enjoy immense independent powers in deciding the fate of a project or a programme.

Assuming that political parties, the civil society and the enlightened members of the public are serious about removing the worst forms of poverty and deprivation, it is necessary to partially replace the notion of 'collective responsibility' of ministers by the notion of 'individual' responsibility in selected areas of particular interest to the public (such as rural development, primary education, employment and infrastructure, etc.). The doctrine of collective responsibility can continue to prevail for all other political purposes, including the continuation of a government in office. Thus, where there is a shortfall in performance of more than the agreed percentage (say, 15 or 20 per cent) in relation to the announced target in the designated area, then the minister concerned must be held responsible, and expected to relinquish office for at least one year.

So far as the civil service structure is concerned, taking into account past experience and the failure to implement the reports and recommendations of numerous commissions, study groups and committees, it is necessary to recognize that it is simply not feasible to reform the system from *within*. The only solution is to reduce the direct role of the bureaucracy in the management of public services. International experience in the management of public services shows that delivery of services can be vastly improved if a distinction is made between the ownership of these services (by the government) and the delivery of such services (by private and local enterprises). Thus, a compilation of twenty-four case studies from twelve countries all over the world has concluded that in every case where the management of a public service was contracted out to private groups or enterprises, the distribution and quality of the service improved and the net cost to the public was reduced. In India also, there are successful examples of 'micro-privatization' (such as Sulabh Sauchalayas and Public Call Offices). These initiatives need to be replicated in respect of other services.

In addition to the need for improving the administrative system for delivery of public services, there is the larger question of the reform of the civil service apparatus for better governance of the country. The most critical issue which needs to be tackled is the 'motivational' issue at the higher levels of the civil services. With frequency of transfers at very short notice at the instance of ministers, the common view in the civil service now is that in order to survive, it is best to conform to ministerial wishes, however unjustified. It is necessary to lay down some transparent ground rules for transfers of civil servants before three or five years in a particular post. *Within* the executive branch, there is also the need for 'separation of powers' between ministers and civil servants in so far as postings, transfers, promotions and other administrative matters are concerned. The civil service is now completely dependent on the pleasure of the ministers even in regard to the most routine administrative matters. It is necessary to reverse this process and confer greater authority on the civil service for self-regulation. The greater empowerment of the civil service must, of course, go hand in hand with greater accountability of civil servants for their performance and ethical conduct. This issue is considered in the chapter 'The supply and demand of corruption'.

It is sad, to say the least, that a country with India's rich cultural heritage and political history is now ranked among the most corrupt countries in the world. Regrettably, there is also widespread public acceptance of corruption as an unavoidable aspect of Indian life. It is not widely realized, however, that corruption is one of the primary reasons for low productivity of investments, fiscal drain and continued mass poverty. High corruption is associated with the wrong choice of high-cost public projects, low maintenance expenditure and poor quality of essential public infrastructure which, in turn, increases the cost of production of goods and services by business enterprises, both public and private.

An important finding of empirical research is that the adverse effects of corruption are more pronounced on small enterprises and growth of employment in the economy. Thus, a survey of 3000 enterprises across twenty transition economies, covering all regions, found that corruption and anti-competitive practices were perceived as the most difficult obstacles by start-up firms. For small enterprises, such practices raised costs and reduced profits because they had to make payments that did not contribute to productivity or output but were necessary for survival. In order to avoid undue harassment, bribes amounting to a substantial portion of the operating costs had to be paid to meet the demands of a host of inspectors working in concert with each other.

To improve productivity, reduce incentives for launching high-cost projects, and alleviate poverty, a multi-pronged strategy to reduce the scope for corruption is now an urgent necessity. An effective strategy would need to focus on institutional reform as well as on reducing the 'demand' and 'supply' of corruption. On the institutional side, there are multiple investigating and prosecution agencies at the centre and in the states to fight corruption. However, while a large number of cases are under investigation at any point of time, the success in prosecuting and punishing the guilty is conspicuous by its absence. In fact, the multiplicity of agencies and the ease with which investigations can be launched without the need to complete them, are among the important causes of the ineffectiveness of anti-corruption measures. An essential component of an anti-corruption strategy is a reduction in the number of agencies involved in investigation and the number of cases that these agencies are expected to investigate. No more than a handful of major cases should be referred for investigation, and the agencies involved should have sufficient access to funds and technical expertise to launch prosecution within ninety days of receiving a major complaint. The objective should be to provide deterrence and exemplary punishment in a few cases rather than investigate a multitude of cases without any result.

The 'supply' of corruption from the top to the bottom of the administrative structure is plentiful. In order to reduce the supply of corruption, it is necessary to reduce the protection provided to government servants and other public functionaries under the Constitution and various judicial pronouncements. Two statutory provisions, among several others, which deserve to be amended forthwith are: Article 311 of the Constitution of India and the Official Secrets Act (1923). Article 311, and the subsequent judicial verdicts, provide virtually unlimited protection to corrupt civil servants because of elaborate and complicated legal requirements before such an official can be reduced in rank, let alone dismissed from service or sent to prison. In order to reduce the level of protection provided to civil servants, it is essential to remove all cases of corruption from the purview of Article 311. This is the minimum that should be done. So far as the antiquated Official Secrets Act is concerned, it is now an opportune time to withdraw it altogether. The Act empowers the government and its officers to classify any document as being secret or top secret, including administrative files. The incentive for corrupt practices, with official secrecy, has increased substantially with increase in political instability in recent years. While the supply of corruption may still be plentiful, there is no need to sanctify it by providing the official veil of secrecy. So far as national security or anti-terrorism activities are concerned, sufficient legislative protection is already available under various other legislative enactments. For example, in 2002, the then government had enacted the Prevention of Terrorism Act, which provided practically unlimited discretion to government officials to prevent any suspected terrorist action without the need to provide sufficient evidence or disclose any specific documents. In 2004, this Act was replaced by the Unlawful Activities (Prevention) Amendment Act, which also provides similar additional protection to government servants (in addition to other long-standing laws which confer special powers on police officers, army and other public servants in the discharge of their duty).

Another vital area on the 'supply' side which requires immediate legislative action is State funding of political parties. The matter has often been discussed but no feasible and politically acceptable consensus has emerged. While recognizing that an equitable formula for allocation of budgetary funds among multiple parties of different sizes is intrinsically difficult, it should still be possible to evolve a formula that is fair and reasonable. Some suggestions to this effect are made in the book. What is necessary now is to find the necessary political will to move in this direction.

The demand for corruption has a 'retail' component and a 'wholesale' component. The retail component consists of the demand generated by individuals who require various kinds of permissions to carry on with the ordinary business of life. The wholesale component is generated by self-seeking corporates and businesses to take advantage of a restrictive practice or price control for their profit. With liberalization of the economy, the demand for wholesale corruption has been reduced, but it is still quite high because of a large number of clearances that are required at various levels, and the large number of ministries and agencies that are involved in providing such permissions.

In order to curb the demand for corruption, the most immediate priority is to 'outsource' and decentralize the system of providing various kinds of licences, registration and permissions to the general public. A recent example of such outsourcing in a routine and simple matter, which has substantially reduced petty corruption and delays, is the decision by the Income Tax Department to delegate the responsibility for issuing Permanent Account Numbers (PAN) to the Unit Trust of India. Further outsourcing of such routine functions among different autonomous agencies can lead to greater accountability and responsiveness to the needs of the public, and thus help reduce corruption. Similarly, in order to reduce the wholesale component in the demand for corruption, it is essential to simplify administrative procedures, reduce the number of governmental agencies involved in providing clearances, and rely on self-certification (with adequate safeguards) by corporates and businesses on compliance with regulatory and legal requirements. The procedural simplification introduced in the last few years in foreign exchange transactions, and elimination of the need for case-by-case clearances, has virtually eliminated corruption in such transactions. A few years ago, this was an area where corruption was rampant. The illegal market in foreign exchange has also virtually disappeared.

I have confined my suggestions to reduce the supply and demand of corruption to only a few core areas (including the need to provide political funding of elections, reduce the scope for administrative and ministerial discretion and simplify the tax system) rather than try and cover the whole gamut of issues that require attention. In particular, for the administration to work with accountability, we urgently need legal reforms that focus sharply on the interests of the public and not only on those of the public servant. Clear mechanisms for establishing accountability for performance are essential, and all forms of special protection for persons working in the government or public sector agencies (except for the armed forces or agencies engaged in the maintenance of law and order) deserve to be eliminated.

A great deal needs to be done to improve the governance system and reduce corruption in the country. If we succeed in reducing administrative complexity and political discretion, the rest will be relatively easy to accomplish.

The Reform of Politics

The last chapter, before the epilogue, is on the urgent need for political reforms. From time to time, in the light of experience and changing circumstances, a need has been felt for constitutional and legislative reforms in the country. A Constitutional Reforms Commission, set up under the chairmanship of Justice Venkatachaliah in February 2000, submitted its report in March 2002.[6] This report is still under consideration by the government; in all probability it will be shelved, as a political consensus on several of its recommendations is unlikely.

My specific suggestions for political reforms are relatively modest but by no means easy to implement. The scope of this section is restricted to only those measures that will make the functioning of the economy more efficient and that will ensure greater accountability of the political leadership for the delivery of public services. An important priority for the future is to further reduce the political role of the government in the economy. While final decisions on policy matters must continue to be made by political authorities, there should be a clear distinction between decisions on policy and their implementation. Once policy decisions have been made, their implementation has to be left to professional administrators without political interference but with due accountability. To make such a division of responsibility work, it is essential to avoid governmental micromanagement and remove procedural bottlenecks. The scope for political or administrative discretion must be eliminated except in a very few large cases which have economy-wide implications. Similarly, in the interest of transparency, there should be full disclosure of the financial decisions made by political authorities on a frequent basis.

A related political imperative is the need for a joint agreement between leaders of major political parties and the trade unions of government employees to improve public services. The cooperation of government employees engaged in delivering public services is essential, and such cooperation is not likely to be forthcoming unless leaders of the leading trade unions give their unqualified support to holding government employees responsible for their performance. A political campaign, with the support of civil society organizations, is now necessary to make the government and public servants more responsive to the needs of the ordinary citizen. There is also a strong case for reducing the number of ministries and governmental organizations involved in implementing anti-poverty and other programmes. In the year 2004, some state governments have nearly a hundred ministers and the central government has sixty-six ministers. A recent legislative amendment to reduce the size of ministries to 15 per cent of the number of legislators is a welcome step, but even this limit is too high for the centre and most states.

An important area where political reform is urgent is regarding the role of small parties, with a handful of members in Parliament or state legislatures, in determining a government's economic agenda. Some of these parties, with less than 5 per cent of the national votes and even a smaller number of members in Parliament can, under certain circumstances, exercise a disproportionate influence in the government and pursue their own agenda. This is contrary to what was envisaged in the Constitution and deserves to be set right. One measure which deserves consideration is to make a legislative provision to the effect that no party which has less than 10 per cent of the members in the Lok Sabha can be part of the government unless it drops its separate identity as a party at the Centre, and joins the main party in a coalition as an associate or an affiliate member until the next elections. If such parties prefer to maintain their separate identity, they can always choose to support the government from outside. Similarly, it may be prescribed that the largest party in a coalition government, along with its pre-poll partners with a common programme, must have a minimum number of seats in the Lok Sabha so that it has a reasonable chance of implementing the programme announced by it during the electoral campaign.

The growing trend towards concentration of powers in the hands of a small number of party leaders and the lack of inner-party democracy among parties large and small is nowhere more evident than in the process of elections to the Rajya Sabha, the Council of States. Members of the state legislatures have no alternative but to blindly vote for the candidates nominated by their parties. A recent legislative amendment, which requires open voting (rather than secret voting) by legislators during elections to the Rajya Sabha, has further strengthened the power of party leaders.

Above all, in a representative democracy like India's, it

is essential to strengthen the role of Parliament, and the authority of the Speaker of Lok Sabha and Chairman of Rajya Sabha in the orderly conduct of business in the two Houses. The shrinking role of Parliament in the functioning of India's democracy was eloquently demonstrated on 26 August 2004, when contrary to convention and well-established rules of procedure, Parliament decided to suspend the question hour, and pass the regular budget involving an expenditure of more than Rs. 4,75,000 crore, and the Finance Bill without any discussion, within a few minutes. This was the result of a backroom agreement between the leaders of parties in the government and the opposition, following several days of disruption of parliamentary work because of a dispute on a sensitive, but extraneous, matter. The Speaker or the Chairman had no alternative but to go along with their decision.

The events of 26 August 2004 constituted a new low in the working of India's democratic institutions. It is necessary now to take immediate legislative measures to avoid a recurrence of similar situations. It may be specifically provided, by legislation, that either House of Parliament cannot be adjourned more than twice in a week unless the listed business, including carried-over business from previous sessions, has been completed. To ensure proper conduct of parliamentary business, the leaders of the two Houses and the leaders of the opposition may be required to nominate two persons as 'whips' from their respective parties who would be charged with the responsibility of ensuring that their members do not continue to disrupt the House beyond prescribed limits. Ad hoc and sudden suspension of rules of business must be eschewed except in an Emergency.

I have no illusion that these and some other changes which have been suggested to make the political system more accountable and strengthen the democratic process would enjoy the support of major parties or their leaders. However, I believe that this is a minimum agenda which deserves consideration and debate in Parliament and outside.

Concluding Observation

My first comprehensive attempt to take a look at India's post-independence economic policies and their outcome was undertaken in a book published in mid-1991, when India was in the middle of a deep economic crisis.[7] This book had gone to press *before* the general elections of May–June 1991, and before the new government announced a set of policies to tackle the crisis. My last book on India was published in 2002, with a couple of other books in-between (in 1992 and 1996).[8]

By the mid-1990s India had successfully embarked on a programme of economic reforms and, for the first time after 1956, achieved security in its balance of payments position. Before I conclude this introductory chapter, it is perhaps useful to look at India's economic situation in the light of the long-term perspective outlined in *India's Economic Crisis*, and updated in later books.

As I look back to 1991 and the developments since then in India and abroad, two facts about the evolution of India's economic policies are striking. The first is that India was able to avoid the recurrence of a crisis during the decade of the 1990s, when a number of robust and fast-growing developing and other countries experienced their worst financial crises. This group of countries includes Mexico (1992 and 1995), Argentina (1995 and 2001), Brazil (1998), Russia (1998) and, of course, the East Asian countries (1997) and Japan. In my view, the reason why India, despite its relatively weak economy, was able to avoid a financial crisis in the 1990s was its ability to undertake reforms with caution and pragmatism, without falling into the trap of 'ideological certainty' and making changes (such as capital account convertibility under conditions of global volatile exchange rate regimes) advocated by many distinguished experts and international institutions. India was quick to realize that while the integration of global financial markets and advances in technology provided substantial new opportunities, developing countries had also become subject to greater vulnerability and external shocks. Strong fundamentals alone could not provide full immunity from a crisis. There was a need to take early preventive action, to build firewalls, and to keep some safety nets handy. India, therefore, took a number of measures to minimize its vulnerability to external crises. These policies proved highly successful, and by the end of the decade, India emerged as a country with one of the strongest external sectors in the developing world.

The second striking fact about the evolution of India's economic policies in the 1990s is that, despite its record of successful macroeconomic management, India was unable to make much progress in the areas of institutional and administrative reforms, which were vital for sustainable high growth. In *India's Economic Crisis* I had proposed a ten-point programme of action for accelerating India's growth and development on a sustainable basis. This programme had included policy proposals to improve external and domestic competition (for example, by abolishing the then prevailing industrial licensing system); eliminate direct physical controls on production and trade; impose a 'hard budget' constraint on public sector enterprises (so that the losses of public sector enterprises are not financed by the government); reduce fiscal deficit; and improve balance of payments viability by adopting a realistic exchange rate policy and shifting the incentive structure in favour of exports. With the exception of fiscal deficits, it is perhaps reasonable to say that in all these areas the progress of reforms in the past decade has been noteworthy and the results have been better than expected.

In addition to these policy measures, the proposed programme of action had also highlighted the urgent need to decentralize the decision-making processes from secretariats and ministries to local institutions and enterprises; reduce the size of the State; make the administrative system more functional; and achieve full literacy by the end of the 1990s. Progress in these areas has not taken place. The main task before us, even after so many years, continues to be the need to launch a bold programme of reforms in the role of the State and the governance structure.

Towards the end of the twentieth century, there were two interesting prognostications about India's potential. The first was by a professor of business management in the United States (Rosenweig 1998).[9] He estimated that by 2025, India would be the third largest economy in the world (after the U.S. and China). The second projection was by a well-known Indian economist (Parikh 1999).[10] It was projected that India would reach a per capita income of U.S.$ 30,000 or higher by 2047, making it one of the fastest growing countries in the world. The projections were unusual at that time, but with the upsurge in the growth rate, similar projections about India's potential have become commonplace (for example, see Rodrik and Subramaniam 2004).[11]

The confidence about India's economic prospects is gratifying. There is no doubt that India now has an opportunity to achieve high growth and remove the worst forms of poverty in the foreseeable future. At the same time, it is useful to remind ourselves that this is not the first time that India's economic prospects are considered to be highly positive. In the early 1950s, soon after independence, India had won worldwide admiration for initiating the process of development planning within a democratic framework. Similarly, in the early 1970s (after the Bangladesh War), and in the mid-1980s (with the resurgence of savings and investment) India was believed to have entered a new growth path. However, these new opportunities did not last long, and the economy was plunged into prolonged crises after some time. The fundamentals are no doubt stronger now, but, as elaborated in subsequent chapters, India faces several old and new challenges in the areas of politics, economics and governance. These challenges can only be met if we are able to generate sufficient political will to pursue the right policies and shake off the deadweight of the past. My fervent hope is that India's participative and democratic system will ensure that corrective action to make India's economy stronger and its politics more people-oriented will be forthcoming sooner rather than later.

References

1. Myrdal, Gunnar (1957), *Economic Theory and Underdeveloped Regions*, Methuen & Co., London, p.viii.

2. Little, I.M.D. (2003), '*Ethics, Economics and Politics: Principles of Public Policy*', Oxford University Press, New Delhi.

3. Mehta, P.B. (2003), *The Burden of Democracy*, Penguin, New Delhi.

4. Centre for Civil Society (2004), *The State of Governance: Delhi Citizen Handbook 2003*, New Delhi.

5. Misra, Rajiv et al. (2003), *India Health Report*, Oxford University Press, New Delhi.

6. Report of the National Commission to Review the Working of the Constitution (2002), Universal Law Publishing Company, Delhi.

7. Jalan, Bimal (1991), *India's Economic Crisis: The Way Ahead*, Oxford University Press, New Delhi.

8. Jalan, Bimal (2002), *India's Economy in the New Millennium*, UBS Publishers, New Delhi; *The Indian Economy: Problems and Prospects*, Penguin-Viking, 1992; *India's Economic Policy: Preparing for the 21st Century*, Penguin-Viking, 1996.

9. Rosenweig, J.A. (1998), *Winning the Global Game*, The Free Press, New York.

10. Parikh, K. (1999), *Economy in India Briefing: A Transformative Fifty Years*, published by M.E. Sharp Inc., New York for Asia Society.

11. Rodrik, D. and Subramaniam, A. (2004), 'Why India Can Grow at 7% a Year or More', *Economic and Political Weekly*, 17–23 April 2004.

ONE

The Triumph and Travails of Democracy

The view of India's democracy among its citizens is somewhat schizophrenic. Most of us admire the democratic system, enjoy our political freedom, and cherish the ability to choose our representatives in Parliament and elected bodies. At the same time, we are wary of the politicians whom we elect and distrust the gargantuan civil service apparatus that we have set up. We are also highly critical of the functioning of many of our public institutions. There are good reasons for both the negative and the positive views about India's democracy as it has evolved since independence. Let me begin with the positives first.

The Rewards of Freedom

Without doubt, India's democratic politics has some highly positive features. Irrespective of caste, creed, religion, the level of income or well-being, the people of India enjoy all basic human freedoms as a matter of right. Elections to local bodies, state legislatures, and Parliament are, broadly speaking, also free and fair. Governments have to seek periodic mandates from the people, and, if voted out, they peacefully yield their place to new governments, which may have similar or radically different agendas. The people's political power was convincingly demonstrated during the 2004 general elections when, contrary to expectations and the survey results of all opinion and exit polls, the government in power lost and a new coalition government of parties that were earlier in opposition was sworn into office within a few days.

Interestingly, despite a vigorous campaign, huge electoral expenditures and governmental backing, more than one-third of the MPs of the ruling coalition lost their seats. A large number of new members were elected, some who were relatively young with no previous electoral experience, some who had lost earlier elections, and some who moved from local or state assemblies to Parliament. The change in the regional balance was also striking. Some of the states, particularly the southern states, which earlier had relatively low representation in the government, became critically important in determining the shape and size of the new cabinet. The biggest surprise was the choice of the new prime minister. A distinguished economist with strong reformist credentials and a reputation for integrity was selected to head the government by a multi-party coalition with the outside support of the Communist parties. The process, the outcome and the whole drama leading to the formation of the new government in 2004 is truly a triumph of India's democracy.

To fully fathom the significance of peaceful transfer of power through periodic elections, it is necessary to recall that at the time of independence, there was worldwide scepticism about the future of India as a united democratic republic. India had, then, 'an untried government, an undigested partition and unclear political alignments, combined with widespread communal violence and social disorder' (Sen 1999).[1] Considering its immense regional, linguistic and religious diversity, it was feared that India would soon break up or at least go back to an authoritarian regime of some kind. But India has not only survived as a democracy, it has emerged as one of the fastest growing developing countries with strong social, cultural and economic bonds across regions. There have been divisive and strong political differences among constituents, but these have largely been tackled within the framework of constitutional procedures. Governments have yielded power according to electoral and parliamentary rules, which gave supremacy to the people. Thus, 'India, an ungainly, unlikely, inelegant combination of differences survives and functions remarkably well as a political unit with a democratic system—indeed held together by its working democracy' (Sen 1999).[2]

The triumph of India's democratic politics is now acknowledged throughout the world. In the words of a distinguished American political scientist:

> India, as an ancient and at once diverse and somehow unified civilization of more than one billion people, deserves recognition for making steady progress under democratic governance without trampling on its neighbours. India achieves greatness by maintaining a democratic rule-of-law government and living in relative peace. India achieves greatness by improving the quality of life of its free citizens.[3]

Nevertheless, there is still considerable debate and some doubts among political theorists and economic experts about the real benefits of democracy for its people. In India, one of the poorest countries in the world, economic progress has been slower than in several authoritarian countries (such as South Korea, Singapore or, for that matter, China). It has been argued that, while democracy is fine in principle, the actual working of democratic politics in India has resulted in generating many problems and rather few solutions (see, for example, Zakaria 2003).[4]

It cannot be denied that economic progress has been slower than warranted. Nor can one overlook the tensions, conflicts and violence that have marked India's political landscape. However, the real question that we need to ponder is not whether democracy has yielded its due rewards to the people, but whether a more authoritarian system would have given better results. On this score, the verdict of history is clear and unequivocal—at least for countries with India's diversity and history of long struggle for freedom from colonial rule. As Amartya Sen has so powerfully argued, the rewards of democracy cannot be evaluated in primarily instrumental terms. For the people of India, freedom and civil rights have an importance of their own.[5] For them, the value of freedom is not necessarily related, directly or indirectly, to its contribution to economic growth or to other social or economic achievements. Democracy is its own reward, and it would be a mistake to treat Indian democracy as a failure on the grounds that it has not helped to generate as high a rate of growth as more authoritarian regimes in a few countries.

Research has also established that there is no direct connection between economic prosperity and authoritarian governance and the suppression of political and civil rights. The experience of some countries, such as Zimbabwe, which has experienced sharp declines in incomes under an authoritarian regime, is a testimony to this fact. The number of dictatorial regimes that have experienced economic deprivation and disasters is as large, if not larger, than democratic regimes. On balance, as extensive inter-country comparison has revealed, the hypothesis that democracy leads to weaker growth is not tenable (Przeworski 1995, Barro 1996).[6] Since political freedom has a value of its own, the case for it remains unaffected despite a democratic country showing a lower rate of growth.

It is also important to note that the policies and circumstances that led to economic success in some authoritarian regimes such as those in South-east Asia in the 1970s or 1980s are not intrinsically related to the nature of their regimes. They are eminently replicable in democratic countries, as India's experience in the 1990s shows. Constructive policies for higher growth (for example, openness to competition, literacy, health, industrial liberalization and export-orientation) can be pursued as effectively in a democracy as in non-democracies, if the government so desires. Thus, India's policies to achieve external viability and a strong balance of payments position in the 1990s have been as successful as policies in East Asia before and after the crisis of 1997. India was also able to achieve a higher rate of growth despite the pace of reforms being slower. East Asian countries are also freer and more democratic in the post-crisis period than before. The change in the nature of their regimes has not hurt their growth or external viability.

An important benefit of democratic functioning and free speech is that, if wrong policies are followed, a correction of these policies is easier and unavoidable in view of public pressure and open discussion. Correcting unviable policies can be delayed, but it cannot be avoided altogether. Similarly, it becomes difficult and untenable for a democratically elected government to ignore the suffering of the people due to droughts or floods, which are quite common in developing countries such as India, and where a large proportion of the population is dependent on agriculture. The role of democracy in preventing famines has also received considerable attention in this context. Thus, it is noteworthy that India has not had a real famine since independence despite endemic undernourishment and malnutrition. China, on the other hand, had the largest famine in recorded history during 1958–61, when wrong public policies led to disastrous results. The authoritarian government was able to continue with its policies, despite widespread starvation, for as long as three years. As a result, nearly thirty million people died for lack of food. This could not have occurred in a country with a free press. The benefits of democracy are therefore clearly apparent both in terms of what it has been able to achieve, and, even more important, in what it has been able to prevent. Similarly, democracy may not be a necessary or an essential condition for high growth, but it is certainly as capable of generating high growth as any other political regime.

For all these reasons, there is no doubt that given a choice, people all over the world are likely to prefer a democratic regime to a non-democratic one. At the same time, it must be emphasized that political freedoms and liberties are permissive advantages and their effectiveness depends crucially on how they are exercised. This is an extremely important point in the context of India's experience in the working of its democratic institutions. Once again, I can do no better than quote Amartya Sen, who has done more to enrich our understanding of the advantages of democracy and the obligation of citizens to derive maximum benefit from it through constant vigilance. Sen observes: 'Democracy does not serve as an automatic remedy of ailments as quinine works to remedy malaria. The opportunity it opens up has to be positively grabbed in order to achieve the desired effect.'[7]

The achievements of democracy depend not only on the rules and procedures that are adopted and safeguarded, but also on the way the opportunities are used by the government in response to popular pressure. Democratic institutions are no doubt important in the functioning of a democracy; however, they should not be viewed as merely mechanical devices for development. Their successful use is dependent on societal value and priorities, and effective public participation in ensuring the accountability of the governance structure. In this context, the roles of political parties and organized opposition groups are particularly vital.

In the following sections, we will deal at greater length with the inadequacies in the working of India's important democratic institutions and their failure to deliver sufficient benefits to which the people are entitled. For example, India's success in eradicating famines is not matched by that in eliminating regular undernutrition, or curing persistent illiteracy or gender inequalities. While the plight of the poor is easy to politicize when there are severe droughts and floods, these other deprivations do not generate as much political excitement. Corrective action is feasible only if there is more effective political participation by the ordinary citizen—in short, fuller practice of democracy. Unfortunately, successive opposition parties have also been relatively reluctant to launch agitations on such vital issues of common concern. Just as it is important to recognize the virtues of democracy, it is also crucial to safeguard the conditions that ensure the range and reach of the democratic process.

A democratically elected government will remain the best option for India, even if the present deficiencies remain unattended. Even in some states, where poor administration and bad governance are the norm, an elected government is a better option over the long term than a non-elected one. India's experience with the Emergency (1975–77) and the widespread abuse of power by persons in authority provide adequate support for this view. However, it is possible to make the democratic system work much better and more effectively for the common person provided we are determined to do so. We should certainly take pride in our democracy, but there can be no room for complacency. Later in this book, I will refer to some of the political reforms that are urgently needed.

The Functioning of India's Democracy

It is perhaps fair to say that in the first fifteen years or so after independence (up to 1962), there was unstinted public support and enthusiasm about the functioning of India's democracy. This was partly due to the charismatic figure of Jawaharlal Nehru. His great qualities of leadership and unflinching devotion to the democratic way of life were abundantly demonstrated during the freedom struggle as well as in the working of India's federal government, Parliament and political parties after independence. Independent India's Constitution was adopted on 26 November 1949, following extensive debate in the Constituent Assembly consisting of all important political leaders, irrespective of party affiliation, and legal luminaries. Within a federal and secular framework, the Constitution gave birth to India's popularly elected Parliament and state legislatures. It also enforced important democratic rights as Fundamental Rights for all its citizens, irrespective of caste, creed and religion. People generally liked what they saw, and for the first time, they were free to say or do what they wished. After two centuries of stagnation, economic backwardness, massive poverty and widespread illiteracy, the development and early industrialization of the country became the primary goal of the nationalist government after independence.

The First Five Year Plan was launched in 1951, followed by the Second Plan in 1956 and the Third Plan in 1961 (and, of course, further five year or annual plans thereafter). The Second Plan was drafted after a nationwide discussion among all stakeholders and academic experts, including distinguished economists from abroad. It was the first exercise of its kind in the world on development planning. The Plan was based on a rigorous analytical framework, which was extensively debated all over the world and emulated by several other developing countries. The State assumed the primary responsibility for the allocation of the country's resources and savings. Backed by the famous model of P.C. Mahalanobis, the well-known statistician, a large number of heavy and other industries were set up (including three steel plants, despite the strong opposition of industrial countries). A vigorous drive for import substitution was undertaken with high levels of protection to overcome the problem of persistent losses in national income arising from a secular decline in the terms of trade of primary commodities during the colonial era.

In the 1950s, the results of planning were also believed to be highly beneficial. There was a vast expansion of India's public sector enterprises ('the temples of modern India', in the famous words of Pandit Nehru). Expansion in the output of capital goods in public enterprises led to a substantial acceleration in the industrial growth to 7 per cent per annum from 1951 to 1961. However, in view of rising trade deficit, mainly because of large imports of capital goods for industrial investments, India's external sector began to show strains culminating in a balance of payments crisis in 1956. As there was worldwide support for India's development strategy, an Aid-India Consortium to increase official and multilateral aid by industrial countries was set up in 1958 under the leadership of the World Bank. This initiative provided immediate relief to cover the balance of payments deficit. India was able to complete the Second Plan in 1961, and proceed with the formulation of the Third Plan. There was some public disappointment about

India running into an external financing problem. However, this was generally believed to be unavoidable for a faster pace of industrialization. The favourable global response in the form of higher aid inflows was also a source of public comfort and reconfirmation of the appropriateness of India's development strategy.

As an integral part of central planning, a strict industrial licensing system was introduced during the 1950s. Controls over imports, which were already in place during the Second World War, were also made more elaborate and comprehensive in order to ensure that scarce foreign exchange was used only for high priority purposes as per the plan. As a result of widespread controls on all transactions and economic activity, bureaucratic corruption, particularly at lower levels of the civil service, was beginning to emerge in ministries involved in issuing permits and licences. In view of high tax rates on personal and corporate incomes (as part of the strategy to mobilize resources for the Plan), tax evasion had also become rampant. An illegal and flourishing market in foreign exchange (in the form of so-called 'Hawala') had also developed by the beginning of the 1960s. Despite these disquieting developments, it is perhaps fair to say that there was no widespread disenchantment with the popularly elected government. Most of the pre-independence leaders, involved in the freedom struggle, were still members of the government and enjoyed wide public support. There were reports of political corruption in some high-profile cases (such as the 'Mundhra scandal' involving investments by the Life Insurance Corporation in companies controlled by the Mundhra group). However, there was as yet no widespread acceptance of corruption in public life. Ministers in charge of the ministries facing serious charges of corruption usually voluntarily resigned from office even before they were chargesheeted, and did not seek re-election until their innocence was established. As a result, there was considerable public confidence about the absence of corruption in the higher echelons of the government and the accountability of ministers.

The Chinese incursions of 1962 and disillusionment with the way the border crisis was handled by the government, including Prime Minister Nehru, perhaps marked a watershed in the people's perception of the working of India's democracy. The planning process was also beginning to show significant strains and the targets set in the Third Plan were beginning to go way off the mark because of lack of resources, increasing bureaucratization of government processes, and poor programme implementation. By the early 1960s, aid flows were stagnant, and the balance of payments position was becoming increasingly unmanageable. In 1965, India faced one of its worst droughts, and several parts of the country were severely affected by starvation. India had to virtually beg for food aid from the United States to prevent famine. As this was also the period of an intense rivalry between the Soviet Union (with whom India had a close relationship) and the United States, the U.S. authorities used this opportunity to derive maximum political leverage. This was followed by the devaluation of the rupee in 1966—a decision believed by many to have been imposed on a helpless and weak India by international financial institutions controlled primarily by the United States. As a result of these and other similar developments, by the end of the 1960s, there was widespread cynicism among the people about the functioning of the government.

The post-1962 period also saw a sharp reduction in industrial and overall growth rates, and the emergence of rampant bureaucratic corruption because of scarcity of foreign exchange and other resources. The demand for foreign exchange, credit and subsidies of various kinds far exceeded supply. Corporates as well as enterprising individuals began to take increasing recourse to corruption in order to get a share of the limited supply of foreign exchange or credit, which were controlled by the government. With the increasing costs of elections and the emergence of a new set of leaders at the Centre and the states, political corruption began to be seen as an inevitable feature of the electoral process.

Notwithstanding these negative developments, there was no strong threat to the stability of the government at the centre, led by the Congress party. The opposition was divided and there did not seem to be any viable alternative. However, the majority of the Congress in Parliament during the 1967 elections was reduced substantially (from 361 members in the Lok Sabha in 1962 to only 283 members in 1967). Even though the growth rate of the economy and the balance of payments situation continued to be weak, during the 1971 elections, the Congress was once again able to command a huge majority (with 352 members in the Lok Sabha). This upsurge in the popularity of the Congress was an outcome of the populist policies promised by the government, and the Indian stance during the Bangladesh war of independence.

Democracy suffered a major blow in 1975, when the Emergency was declared by the government. The fundamental rights of the people were suspended, and democratic institutions, including Parliament, became subservient to the government. Fortunately, the government decided to go for fresh general elections in 1977. The experience of the Emergency and the public indignation that ensued galvanized the opposition parties, and the Congress lost power for the first time after independence. The new Janata Party government restored individual rights as well as the democratic functioning of Parliament and other institutions.

However, because of internal dissensions, the new government did not last long and the Congress came back to power with a large majority in 1980.

The decade of the 1980s was generally good for the functioning of democracy in India. The dictatorial and non-democratic elements in the Congress had suffered a major blow in the 1977 electoral verdict. The failure of the Emergency was a powerful endorsement of the preference for democracy by the people. At the same time, the fact that the government formed by a coalition of regional and minority national parties did not last long gave credence to the view that only the Congress could provide a viable and stable government at the centre. The new government formed by the Congress in 1980 worked reasonably democratically, and a process of reform was also initiated to reduce the control of the government over the economy. Licensing, foreign exchange, credit and capital market control were liberalized. The government also became more open to foreign direct investment, and less inclined to expand the role of the public sector. As a result of these initiatives, there was an upsurge in the growth rate and the domestic economy became stronger. In the second half of the 1980s, there was also, for the first time after more than two decades, an emergence of a surplus in the overall balance of payments, and India was comfortably able to repay its earlier loans from the International Monetary Fund. However, a major corruption scandal (namely, the so-called Bofors scandal relating to purchases of defence equipment) involving the government at the highest level erupted in 1987, and the Congress lost power to a coalition of opposition parties in 1989.

The fifteen-year period since then—from 1989 to 2004—has witnessed considerable political instability, both at the centre and the states with substantial impact on the morale and the style of functioning of political parties. Since 1989, the country has undergone as many as six general elections, and multiple coalitions of different parties have ruled the country. There have been seven prime ministers, five of whom had tenures ranging from a few days to about one year. Prior to 1989, in the first forty-one years of independence, six prime ministers had ruled the country, of whom only three had tenures of less than five years. After the most recent elections in 2004, the coalition that has taken charge is dependent on the support of several parties of the right and the left. A post-election Common Minimum Programme has been adopted backed by all parties supporting the government.

A consequence of the emergence of coalition governments since 1989 has been the expansion in the size of the cabinet on top of a gargantuan civil service. Earlier, with occasional exceptions, cabinets at the centre and in the states used to consist of a body of persons drawn from the majority party in the legislature. In recent years, the size of the cabinets has tended to increase, with representatives of different parties pulling in different directions. The concept of collective responsibility of the cabinet, as enshrined in the Constitution, has weakened, adding to the clumsiness of the governance structure.

In theory, Parliament still continues to be supreme, and the cabinet is certainly accountable to it. In practice, however, the accountability of the executive to Parliament has become perfunctory and pro forma as long as the government has the majority support of a party or a combination of parties. The power of the leader of a party over its members is supreme and unquestioned, and what happens in Parliament now is largely determined by the political interests of different parties rather than by the intrinsic merits or demerits of actions taken by the executive.

As the number of parties involved in forming a government has become larger, there has been increasing politicization in the functioning of all branches of the government. There is little accountability or autonomy of various institutions set up under the Constitution for ensuring equality, social justice and republicanism. Thus, in the executive branch, while the entry into civil services is still largely immune from political pressures, the functioning of the bureaucracy has become highly politicized. Entry into parastatal organizations is also becoming subject to political pressures because of the ability of ministers to create jobs and start projects, irrespective of their viability or need. The politicization of the bureaucracy in recent years has been further exacerbated by more frequent changes of government at the centre and in most of the states. Increasingly, the political leadership is inclined to use its powers to meet its party's immediate political or financial objectives, irrespective of the advice of civil servants.

The judiciary continues to be independent, and its powers of legal adjudication are enormous. However, with a huge proliferation of legal enactments, the judicial system is crumbling under the weight of hundreds and thousands of cases that continue to be filed before it every year. There is now a huge backlog of pending cases, some of which are ten to twenty years old. In some of the courts, it could take more than fifty years to clear this backlog, even if no further cases are filed. The long delays in delivering justice caused a cynic to observe that filing false cases was now the 'last refuge of a scoundrel'! Anyone who is on the wrong side of the law (including criminal or anti-corruption laws) can buy sufficient time and freedom for himself by simply filing cases and appealing to higher and higher levels. The political authorities also have full freedom and the power to keep the judicial system underfunded and understaffed.

The above is a broad synoptic overview of the functioning of India's democracy since independence. To sum up, there seem to be four distinct phases in the functioning of India's democracy since independence. The first fifteen years, up to 1962, generally yielded positive results in strengthening democratic political institutions and generating faster economic growth. The second phase, up to 1979, was volatile in the political sphere. This period saw a suspension of democracy followed by a strengthening of the democratic political processes. Except for some years of high growth, economic growth was, however, low and in the range of 3 to 3.5 per cent with frequent balance of payments crises. The third phase, up to 1989, was generally good for the strengthening of India's democracy as well as the economy. The last phase, since 1989, has seen the emergence of an altogether new scenario of coalition politics of parties with different ideologies. This period has been marked by increasing expectations of political instability and uncertainty, which has had major consequences for the functioning of democratic institutions.

In the following sections of this chapter, an attempt has been made to look a little more closely into the actual functioning of the three vital institutions of India's democracy—Parliament, the permanent bureaucracy and the judiciary—during the recent phase, that is, since 1989. These changes are substantial enough to have wideranging implications for the functioning of India's society, polity and the economy. These developments and their consequences on the lives of ordinary citizens deserve consideration by political observers, experts and commentators. The economic consequences of recent political developments will be discussed in chapter 2.

The Shrinking Role of Parliament

Pratap Bhanu Mehta (2003) has pointed out: 'In most democracies, the groundwork of political education is done within political parties and the more open and democratic their structure, the more likely it is that politicians will be better educated on the issues. More effective forms of accountability and deliberation require a pluralization of the sites at which politicians are held accountable and parties are essential to this process.'[8] Unfortunately, in India, while there has been a proliferation of political parties in the last fifteen years, this has been accompanied by a greater centralization of power in the hands of their leaders. Most parties are now characterized by arbitrariness, haphazardness, lack of deliberative purpose and tolerance for corruption.

The frequency of elections since 1989—six of them—and the expectation that the tenure of a government is going to be short has had several unintended consequences. Ideology and programmes have become relatively less important, and any party (of whatever type) is willing to combine with any other party for possible political or electoral gain. Some parties have split several times to gain temporary electoral advantage, and some parties have moved from one side to another in order to form governments. The number of parties fielding candidates for elections has multiplied, and it is difficult to distinguish among the programmes or ideologies of most parties. As many as fifty-five parties contested the 2004 elections, with various kinds of inter-party alliances. It is doubtful whether the electorate was able to tell which party or combination of parties stood for what kind of programme or vision of an India of the future. There were, of course, different local or even national issues espoused by different parties in different parts of the country. However, it would have been impossible to identify a particular pattern or reason behind a party's choice of issues that deserved its support and issues that did not.

An important consequence of the political instability has been the dominance of smaller parties by a few individuals, and complete absence of intra-party democracy in most parties. Some parties, whether large or small, have only one leader who decides who will be the party's candidates for elections, who will become members of the government led by another party and who will be sent to the Upper House of Parliament. Most of the smaller parties have a narrow social base, but their supreme leaders enjoy considerable political power in view of their ability to swing relatively small numbers of votes in favour of another party, particularly in marginal seats.

The frequent splits among parties, and the tendency among smaller party formations to destabilize governments in office, have been matters of concern for constitutional experts as well as major political parties. A related area of concern has been the process of indirect elections by state legislatures to the Upper House of Parliament (that is, the Rajya Sabha or the council of states). Since voting by legislatures was by secret ballot, in some cases legislators of a particular party in a state assembly voted for a candidate other than the one nominated by their own party. In order to prevent the destabilization of a government by splitting a party in coalition, and to prevent cross-voting during Rajya Sabha elections, two important legislative changes have been adopted by Parliament. The first amendment is that any elected member (or a group of members) who decides to leave his or her party will have to seek fresh election. This amendment more or less ensures that a party cannot be split between elections by any number of disgruntled members. The second amendment (for election to the Rajya Sabha) has replaced secret voting by an open voting process by members of legislatures. This amendment is designed to prevent cross-voting and members who do not vote for their party's candidates may be removed from their party for 'indiscipline'. The domicile requirement of candidates for Rajya Sabha elections has also been removed. Members of the Rajya Sabha no longer have to be residents of the state that elects them.

On the face of it, these amendments seem eminently worthwhile because they are designed to reduce instability and corruption among the members of a party. However, in reality, the effect has been to strengthen the powers of party leaders over their members. The solution adopted, with multi-party consensus, is in fact a lot worse than the disease. There are no longer checks and balances against the decisions of the leader of a party by the members of his or her party. The leader is free to create instability by forcing all members of the party to leave the coalition, even if the majority of the members do not privately agree with the decision. Similarly, nomination to the Rajya Sabha has become the sole prerogative of the leader of a party and a few persons who enjoy his or her confidence. The select few can choose whomsoever they want to send to the Rajya Sabha, including those charged with corruption. Bribery or the funding of parties in exchange for nomination to the Rajya Sabha has also not been curbed. In fact, the new amendment may encourage institutionalized corruption in the nomination process.

While Parliament sessions are held frequently and vast quantities of papers containing information on the working of ministries are placed before it, the role of Parliament in holding the government accountable for its performance has become largely perfunctory. Parliamentary debates have become highly party-political. There is plenty of shouting and frequent walk-outs by parties in the opposition, and charges of corruption and wrongdoing by ministers have become common. However, after the shouting, all that happens is yet another adjournment. Government business or legislative proposals, which require parliamentary approval, are generally approved without much debate and within a few minutes towards the end of the day when few members, including those from the parties in power, are present.

There was a time when assurances given by ministers on the floor of Parliament had a ring of credibility to them. Unlike other commitments, those made in the two Houses were supposed to be translated into reality if only for the fear of attracting breach of privilege proceedings. This is no longer the case. Assurances in Parliament are now just like others, meant to be bypassed without explanation. In 2004, as many as 1337 'assurances' given in the Rajya Sabha and 1630 in the Lok Sabha, some of them more than a decade old, were still pending. With a higher turnover of ministers, nobody takes any responsibility for assurances given by previous ministers.

If proof was needed about how non-functional the Indian Parliament had become, this was amply provided by its proceedings in August 2004. After the new government took office in May 2004, the regular budget session of Parliament was convened in early July. The budget for 2004–05 was presented, and as per past practice, after a general debate, Parliament went into a two-week recess to enable its Standing Committee to have an in-depth discussion of the programmes of various ministries. These committees, on which all political parties were represented, did the work assigned to them and presented their reports for consideration by the two Houses of Parliament. Parliament was then reconvened specifically to discuss the budget proposals and pass the Finance Bill with amendments as appropriate (along with some other important and long-pending legislative business). However, after a day or two of debate on some non-budgetary resolutions, the parliamentary proceedings were heavily disrupted by the opposition on account of their dissatisfaction with the government's position on certain sensitive, but extraneous, matters. Neither House of Parliament was able to conduct any business for several days. And then, all of a sudden, there was a backroom agreement among leaders of the major parties that Parliament should be prorogued one week in advance without any discussion whatsoever of the budget provisions, the Finance Bill, or the reports of Standing Committees. It was also agreed among party leaders that the budget would be passed by a voice vote unanimously within two or three minutes of the meetings of both Houses. Contrary to long-standing rules of parliamentary business, it was also decided by major parties to dispense with the question hour as well as other listed business. On 26 August 2004, both the Houses did exactly what the few party leaders decided, much to the dismay of several of the members and the general public. Some independent members protested, but to no avail. The agreement among parties to dispense with even the most basic constitutional requirement for the passage of the general budget is a sad commentary on the working of India's parliamentary democracy.

The functioning of Parliament and state legislatures in recent years has also been examined in detail by the National Commission to Review the Working of the Constitution. The commission's observations are worth noting:

> If there is a sense of unease with the way the Parliament and the state legislatures are functioning, it may be due to a decline in recent years in both the quantity and quality of work done by them. Over the years the number of days on which the houses sit to transact legislative and other

business has come down very significantly. Even the
relatively fewer days on which the houses meet are often
marked by unseemly incidents, including use of force to
intimidate opponents, shouting and shutting out of debate
and discussion resulting in frequent adjournments. There
is increasing concern about the decline of Parliament,
falling standards of debate, erosion of the moral authority
and prestige of the supreme tribune of the people.[9]

An important initiative was taken in 1993 to improve the
functioning of Parliament by setting up seventeen
Departmental Standing Committees to consider, in depth,
the demands for grants of the ministries and departments
with objectivity and 'freedom from partisan passions'.
Unfortunately, even the work of these Standing Committees
has become largely ceremonial. Plenty of reports are
produced, deficiencies in the working of ministries are
discussed, and a large number of recommendations are
made. But practically no action has been taken by the
government, except to report that 'necessary action is under
consideration'. With increase in political instability, soon a
new government or a new minister takes office, and the
Standing Committees are reconstituted under a new
chairman. In any case, the committees have large membership
(with as many as forty-five members belonging to different
parties). Again, to quote the National Commission, 'the
adhocism (sic) tells on the quality of work done by the
committees whose reports suffer from absence of critical
analysis of the work of the ministries under their supervision.
Parliamentary oversight, essential for enforcing accountability
of the executive, is worse than useless if it degenerates into
a meaningless routine' (p.107).

No wonder then that by and large, the ordinary people
of India are disenchanted with the working of the political
system. They still have the political power to vote or not to

vote, but what their vote does for them is not evident. Political parties are now subservient to their leaders, and not to the people who sustain them.

The Politicization of the Bureaucracy

In order to provide an effective system of governance, India's administrative structure is divided into two parts. At the top of the administrative structure is the political side as represented by the cabinet under the leadership of the prime minister. Then there is the permanent civil service, which is appointed through an open competitive system. Entry into the civil service is open to all eligible Indian citizens irrespective of caste, creed or religion. The selection for the civil service posts at all levels of government at the centre and states is truly independent of political interference. This division of the administrative structure between the political part and the non-political civil service part is expected to ensure that while all policy decisions affecting the public are made by the politicians, the implementation of these policies is carried out by an independent non-political civil service. The separation of the policy-making function from the implementation function is an essential feature of the Constitution as it is expected to provide equality of treatment to all citizens, irrespective of political or party affiliations.

The role of the administrative bureaucracy is necessarily subordinate to that of the political leadership. The government's priorities and its work programme are set by the elected politicians, and the bureaucracy is supposed to ensure that this programme is implemented according to the laws in force and in line with approved administrative procedures. While implementing the programmes set by the cabinet and ministers, bureaucrats are expected to act without fear or favour, and ensure that the benefits of the programmes flow to the people regardless of their political affiliations. While politicians are free to overrule the advice rendered by civil servants, the advisory functions of the bureaucracy are expected to be performed without regard to their impact on the private interests of politicians and the party in power.

In India, slowly but surely, the independent role of the bureaucracy has been seriously compromised over the years. Thus, according to the report of the National Commission to Review the Working of the Constitution, 'arbitrary and questionable methods of appointments, promotions and transfers of officers by political superiors also led to corrosion of the moral basis of its independence. It has strengthened the temptation in the services to collusive practices with politicians to avoid the inconvenience of transfers and for officers to gain advantage by ingratiating themselves to political masters. They would do the politicians' biddings rather than adhere to rules. Lest the situation become more vicious, it is necessary that a better arrangement be conceived under the Constitution.'[10]

Politicization of the bureaucracy in India is primarily the result of governments with short tenures pursuing their private or party interests in the guise of promoting the larger public good. Any party which comes to power tends to appoint pliable bureaucrats who are expected to carry out the wishes of its party leaders, irrespective of their merits or legality. If a bureaucrat does not comply, he or she is likely to be immediately transferred to another position in another location. According to one study, in one year alone, in the state of Uttar Pradesh (when there was a six-monthly rotation of the government headed by the leaders of two parties, BJP and BSP, in coalition), there were 1000 transfers among members of the elite Indian Administrative Service (IAS) and Indian Public Service (IPS). Under one head of government, transfers ran at an average of seven per day.

Under the second head of government, who took office after the expiry of six months, transfers rose to sixteen per day! Thus, over half the corps of IAS officers were transferred within twelve months of posting.[11]

The deleterious effects of frequent transfers on the morale and effectiveness of top civil servants have been enormous. The costs in the loss of quality of administration have also been significant. The civil service has become increasingly weak since there is no time available to a newly appointed civil servant to acquire even the minimum knowledge necessary for an effective discharge of his or her functions. Incompetence at the top leads to acts of passive resistance and delays by subordinates. Corruption becomes unavoidable, both to avoid transfers as well as to get remunerative postings by corrupt officials.

The process of politicization has been further aided and abetted by the trade union organizations of government employees at different levels. The overwhelming majority of civil servants in terms of numbers is in the clerical grades or lower (Class III and Class IV). Their trade unions are affiliated with the central trade unions of major political parties and enjoy tremendous influence, irrespective of which party or parties are in power. All the parties are ostensibly pro-labour and compete for the support of employees' unions and even the most unreasonable demands of government employees are likely to receive a favourable response at the expense of the public. It is ironic that with the opening of the economy and more competitive private sector job markets, most of the strikes by labour unions are now in government and public sector enterprises! The pay scales of government and public sector employees in the clerical and lower grades are two to two and a half times higher than those in the private sector. The demand for creation of more jobs and more pay in the public sector by the employees and their political leaders has naturally become more pervasive over time. There is also a 'quid pro quo'. Political leaders deliver what civil service unions demand by way of pay, security of service, leave, working hours and creation of jobs. In their turn, civil servants deliver what the politicians want in terms of power and favours. The casualty is the public interest.

This, unfortunately, is the true state of affairs in the evolving relationship between the civil service, the government and the people. The triumph of democracy and the power of the people are evident every time elections are held. Between elections, after governments have taken office and political leadership is in control of the civil service, the public interest and norms exist only in their breach. Some suggestions for reforming the civil service and for separating the responsibility of political and bureaucratic sides within the executive branch are made in a later chapter.

An Overburdened Judiciary

India is a federal polity, but unlike many other federations (including that of the United States), there is no separate system of federal and state courts. One system of courts deals with the enforcement of laws—both of the Union and of the states. The Indian judiciary has the ultimate power to interpret and define the scope and limitations of the powers of the executive as well as the legislature under the Constitution. The entry into the judicial service is independent of political authority. While top-level appointments to the Supreme Court of India as well as the high courts are made by the executive branch, the selection is made on the recommendation of the judiciary. Strict rules of procedure and conventions have been established to ensure that appointments to the judiciary at different levels are made according to well-established principles without reference to political considerations.

The judiciary has immense powers of adjudication, and it can declare any law passed by the legislature as being inconsistent with the Constitution and, therefore, invalid. It also has the power to declare any executive action by the political authority or the civil service as being illegal, hence ineffective. Every citizen, or for that matter, any other person (including a non-resident) has the right to approach or to appeal to the courts for a redressal of grievances against executive actions, including those by parastatal organizations.

In addition, a number of civil and other institutions have been set up under the Constitution, or statutes under it, for ensuring social justice and the exercise of fundamental rights by citizens without any interference by political authority. These include various national commissions (such as the Human Rights Commission or the Minorities Commission) and the Central Vigilance Commission to provide equal access to all citizens and to protect them against corrupt practices by politicians or civil servants.

In principle, neither the executive nor Parliament can override a judicial verdict. They can file appeals or request a review of decisions by courts, but they ultimately have to abide by final judicial directions. However, as so often happens in India, public institutions do not quite work the way they are supposed to. An important and positive institutional characteristic can easily be turned into a disadvantage in practice. Thus, easy and equal access to the judicial system—with various levels of appeal—is supposed to ensure that people's fundamental and other rights are fully protected. In practice, however, the maximum advantage of the right to appeal at various levels of the judiciary has been taken by unscrupulous persons, including politicians charged with various crimes, in order to delay the judicial process. A delay of ten to fifteen years in settling even the most blatant and clear-cut legal violation is quite common. The easiest way of deviating from a commercial obligation or a contract is to file a case in a court. As a result, all courts, particularly high courts, are now overburdened with pending cases, and the effectiveness of the judicial system in protecting the rights of the people has been seriously eroded.

Similarly, the independence of the judiciary from the executive and the legislature is expected to insulate the judicial system from political pressure. However, the budgets, salaries, as well as various other infrastructure facilities for the functioning of the judicial system have to be approved by the executive. There are now enormous delays in filling up important vacancies, and most courts are understaffed and inadequately serviced. In line with pre-independence colonial traditions, the courts are generally on vacation for several months in a year, and the disposal of cases is painfully slow. Even in routine matters affecting the ordinary citizen, such as rent control, inheritance disputes or family maintenance, cases filed more than ten years ago are still pending in different courts. The combined effect of the large number of pending cases along with inadequate staffing and insufficient infrastructure facilities has rendered the judicial system largely ineffective in delivering speedy justice.

The problems affecting the judicial system, particularly the question of delay in delivering justice, have been examined from time to time by Law Commissions, Special Committees, and Conferences of Chief Justices. Various recommendations have also been made to improve the situation. However, no effective action has so far been taken, and delays continue to mount.

On the whole, it is perhaps fair to conclude that while there have been ups and downs in the functioning of India's democracy at various times since independence, the more recent period has been particularly awkward. The increase in the frequency of elections and the emergence of unstable governments have had several unintended consequences. Governments with expectations of short tenures have became non-accountable for their performance; the power of small parties and their leaders in coalition governments has increased substantially; and inner-party democracy has virtually disappeared. Political corruption has acquired a new legitimacy as a necessary condition for a coalition government of several parties to remain in power. Bureaucracy has become highly politicized, particularly in states where regional or caste-based parties are dominant. The role of Parliament in ensuring accountability of the government and performance of the ministries has also diminished over time. The judicial system, which otherwise continues to be independent and free from political interference, has become overburdened and less effective.

For the poor in India, a country with one of the lowest per capita incomes in the world, the political system as it has evolved over the past few decades does not have much to offer—except the periodic satisfaction of casting their votes. The freedom to cast his or her vote is no doubt important and worthwhile for every citizen. But this is not enough. The disjuncture between economics and politics in India's democratic system has also been growing. The next chapter deals with this and some other factors which, despite the reforms of the 1990s, are likely to adversely affect India's economic performance in the future.

References

1. Sen, A.K. (1999), *Development as Freedom*, Alfred A. Knopf, New York, p.157.

2. Ibid.

3. Perkovich, G. (2003), 'The Measure of India: What Makes Greatness', Annual Fellows' Lecture, The Centre for the Advanced Study of India, University of Pennsylvania, 23 April 2003, p.17.

4. Zakaria, F. (2003), *The Future of Freedom*, Penguin-Viking, New Delhi.

5. Sen, A.K. (2004), 'Democracy and Secularism in India', in K. Basu (Ed.), *India's Emerging Economy: Performance and Prospects in the 1990s and Beyond*, Oxford University Press, New Delhi.

6. Przeworski, A. (1995), *Sustainable Democracy*, Cambridge University Press, Cambridge. Also, Barro, R.J. (1996), *Getting It Right: Markets and Choices in a Free Society*, The MIT Press, Cambridge, Massachusetts.

7. Sen, A.K., 1999, p.155.

8. Mehta, P.B. (2003), *The Burden of Democracy*, Penguin, New Delhi, p.154.

9. Report of the National Commission to Review the Working of the Constitution (2002), Government of India, New Delhi, p.105.

10. Ibid., p.124.

11. Banik, D. (1999), *The Transfer Raj: Indian Civil Servants on the Move*, Centre for Development and the Environment, Oslo.

TWO

The Economics of Non-performance

At first glance, the title of this chapter may seem odd. In recent years, India has been commended for its excellent economic performance by economists, expert commentators and international agencies. It is one of the fastest growing economies, and there is an emerging consensus that if India follows the right policies, by 2020 or 2025 it will be the third largest economy in the world (see Parikh 1999 or Rosenweig 1998).[1] The optimism about India's growth potential was further strengthened by India's success in avoiding 'contagion' after the 1997 East Asian crisis, which adversely affected a number of other developing countries. Today, India's balance of payments position is stronger than at any time in its post-independence history, and it has one of the highest levels of foreign exchange reserves in the world amounting to $130 billion at the end of 2004.

All this is certainly true. However, as one eminent Indian economist has observed, 'India is notorious for blowing its chances, not only in cricket but also vis-à-vis the economy.'[2] Thus, for example, as far back as 1956, the Second Five Year Plan was launched with great fanfare after considerable debate among leading economists in India and abroad. It was supposed to bring about a transformation in the economy, make India self-reliant, and abolish poverty in twenty-five years, by 1981. However, very soon India was engulfed in a major foreign exchange crisis and remained trapped for the next twenty years in a vicious circle of low growth and high poverty. Similarly, in the early 1980s, with foreign exchange reserves beginning to build up, the savings rate crossing 20 per cent for the first time and the economy running a food surplus, many felt that the time for India's economic take-off had come. However, before the end of the decade, the economy again ran out of steam and in 1990–91 was caught up in yet another serious balance of payments crisis. The new government, which came to power in 1991, launched an impressive programme of economic reforms which yielded results. The industrial licensing system was abolished, foreign exchange controls were liberalized, import tariffs were lowered and the burgeoning fiscal deficit was reduced. During the four-year period of 1993–94 to 1996–97, the growth rate exceeded 7 per cent per annum, and once again there was considerable optimism about India's economic future. However, soon the economy slowed down again and in the first three years of the new millennium (2000–01 to 2002–03), the average growth rate was less than 5 per cent, partly because of the severe drought in 2002–03. The picture changed dramatically once again in 2003–04, and the growth rate was expected to exceed 8 per cent, which was the second highest rate of growth in the world after China, whose growth rate is supposed to be close to 10 per cent.

It is natural to ask—has anything really changed about India's economic prospects, or is the economy likely to continue to swing from a positive to a negative outlook? Naturally there is no unanimous or unequivocal answer to this question (particularly among economists!). My own view is that there is indeed a fundamental change, for the better, in India's global economic position, and opportunities for it to accelerate its rate of growth are truly immense. As I have argued in greater detail elsewhere, in view of the changing role of knowledge-based services (such as professional and information technology services) in overall growth, the sources of comparative advantage of a nation are vastly different today from what they were fifty or even twenty years ago.[3]

There are very few developing countries as well placed as India to take advantage of the phenomenal changes that have occurred in production technologies, international trade, capital movement and deployment of skilled manpower. An important change in production technology from the Indian point of view is the importance of information technology and software in the value of output and productivity in all sectors of the economy, including manufacturing. India today has the knowledge and the skills to produce and process a wide variety of industrial and consumer products and services. Another important factor in India's favour is international capital mobility and the integration of global financial markets. Domestic savings continue to be important for development. However, scarcity of domestic capital is no longer a binding constraint. Increased mobility of capital has ensured that global resources will flow to countries which can show high growth and high returns. It is now possible for India to participate in the virtuous circle of higher growth, higher external capital inflows, and higher domestic incomes and savings, which in turn can lead to further growth.

While there is no doubt about India's immense 'potential', taking advantage of the new opportunities will require a change in the country's vision of the future and its economic strategy. Some changes have no doubt been made in this direction, particularly in the 1990s, but much still remains to be done. On present reckoning, and keeping in view the complex political scenario as it has evolved during the past decade, it is not yet clear that economic performance in the foreseeable future will significantly exceed the post-1980s trend rate of growth. The peformance of the economy in recent years has been certainly much better than what was achieved in the previous three decades (less than 4 per cent per annum), but it is certainly well below India's potential. If India were prepared to grasp the opportunities that are now available, the trend rate of growth could be at least two percentage points higher (that is, 8 per cent per annum or more). There are, however, three important factors which may impede or delay the realization of its full economic potential. These are:

- the deadweight of the past in our economic vision and strategy;
- fiscal disempowerment, largely due to the power of 'distributional coalitions'; and
- the growing 'disjuncture' between economics and politics in public life.

In the rest of this chapter, an attempt is made to assess the likely impact of these factors on India's economic outlook.

The Deadweight of the Past

The reasons for India opting for a highly controlled state-dominated development strategy after independence in 1947 are well known. The economic profile of the country at that time was distressing. There was hardly any growth in the previous half-century, and both agriculture and industry were characterized by severe structural distortions. Like other underdeveloped countries, India was an exporter of cheap primary products and an importer of industrial products with secular decline in its terms of trade and stagnation in per capita incomes. During the first half of this century, the rate of growth of national income was at less than 1 per cent per year which was comparable to the rate of population growth during this period. In real terms, therefore, at the time of independence, the average Indian was as badly off as he or she had been at the turn of the century. Against this background, there was unanimity among nationalist intellectuals, political leaders and industrialists about the preferred directions of economic strategy after independence (Chandra 1992).[4] The need for the government to occupy the commanding heights and to lead from the top received further support from the astounding success of the erstwhile Soviet Union in emerging as a rival centre to the West of political and industrial power within a very short period. India at that time played a pioneering role in giving expression to the aspirations of the newly independent Third World countries in the economic field. Following the example of the Soviet Union, there was also a broad consensus on many of the strategic issues, such as the vital role of the public sector, the discouragement of foreign investment, the development of heavy industries and the need for centralized allocation of resources.

While the reasons for adopting a centrally directed strategy of development were understandable against the background of colonial rule, it soon became clear that the actual results of this strategy were far below expectations. Instead of showing high growth, high public savings and a high degree of self-reliance, India was actually showing one of the lowest rates of growth in the developing world, with rising public deficits and periodic balance of payments crises. According to one calculation, in thirty out of the forty years between 1950 and 1990, India had balance of payments problems of varying intensity. Looking back, it is hard to believe that for as long as four decades after 1950, India's growth rate averaged less than 4 per cent per annum, and the per capita income growth was less than 2 per cent per annum. This was at a time when the developing world, including Sub-Saharan Africa and other least developed countries, showed a growth rate of 5.2 per cent per annum.

However, the most striking failure was not in terms of growth, or even in the precarious situation of the balance of payments. Although the argument is not convincing, it could still be claimed that the low growth outcome was on account of a number of factors beyond India's control, such as the border wars, severe droughts, periodic oil shocks and, finally, the inhospitable global environment! The balance of payments difficulties could also—with some imagination—be attributed to the global woes of primary producers, and the struggle of a poor developing country like India to industrialize and become self-reliant in heavy industry (which previously had been the monopoly of the rich industrialized countries). The most conspicuous failure for which there is no alibi, and the responsibility for which lies squarely and indisputably at our door, is the erosion in public savings and the inability of the public sector to generate resources for investment or the provision of public services.

It will be recalled that an important assumption in the choice of post-independence development strategy was the generation of public savings, which could be used for higher and higher levels of investment. However, this did not happen, and the public sector, instead of being a generator of savings for the community's good, became a consumer of the community's savings. This reversal in roles had become evident by the early 1970s, and the process reached its culmination by the early 1980s. By then the government had begun to borrow not only to meet its own revenue expenditure, but also to finance public sector deficits and investments. During the period 1960 to 1975, total public sector borrowings (including government borrowings) averaged 4.4 per cent of GDP. These increased to 6 per cent of GDP by 1980–81, and further to 9 per cent by 1989–90.

Thus, the public sector, which had a commanding

presence in almost all industrial sectors of the economy, particularly heavy industry, gradually became a net drain on the society as a whole. It is interesting to note that the central government's total internal public debt reached a stupendous Rs. 5,00,000 crore by the mid-1990s, and nearly one-third of it was accounted for by assets held in the public sector. Interest payments on public debt at that time amounted to nearly Rs. 40,000 crore, which were financed by new net borrowings and represented nearly 70 per cent of the centre's fiscal deficit. In effect, one-third of the interest payments was on account of the government's past investment in the public sector. By the end of the 1990s, the Centre's internal debt almost doubled, to Rs. 9,70,000 crore. This sharp increase was partly accounted for by the need to borrow higher and higher amounts to service the debt.

Looking back at the performance of the public sector in contributing to national savings (which has been negative for the past three decades), it is amazing how much of the economic and political debate on future strategy is still conditioned by the pre-1947 colonial experience and special interests. Irrespective of which party or coalition of parties is in power, political leaders (with very few exceptions) express their confidence in the ability of the public sector to generate savings. Disinvestment targets, particularly for loss-making units, may be announced from time to time, but are unlikely to be reached. From time to time, the ministers in charge of loss-making public sector units also announce their intentions to revive these units by making further investments, even though they are fully aware of the dismal record of such efforts (Acharya 2004, Panagariya 2004).[5]

I should make it clear that the issue here is not public sector vs. private sector or the ideological predilections in favour of state-dominated development strategy vis-à-vis market-dominated strategy. Nor is it about the virtues of globalization or its discontents. The issue is simply about proper uses of national savings in an environment of rising fiscal deficits. Is it appropriate to use these savings for financing further losses of public sector units which are of no particular interest or service to the vast majority of India's poor? Is it appropriate to continue with vast and rising government borrowings and the disproportionate burden of interest payments on the government's budget when earlier borrowings invested in the public sector were not giving adequate returns? There is no doubt that the financial interests of workers in the public sector, whether these units are yielding returns or not, deserve to be protected. The crucial issue is whether the most economically efficient way of protecting these interests is through further government borrowings for financing mounting losses and low returns in these units? Or, whether these interests can be adequately protected through a more productive use of the capital (including land) that is locked up in these units?

At this point, it can be argued that what is needed is better and more professional management by reducing political/bureaucratic control of public enterprises. Several government committees over the past three decades have made recommendations along the same lines, which have been accepted by the government 'in principle'. Some ministries also tried to implement these recommendations, and achieved some success—for a while. However, with the change in government or ministers (who generally have even shorter tenures than the government because of cabinet reshuffles), uncertainty and drift is likely to continue. It is better to recognize this political reality rather than evade it in considering the options. Another factor which needs to be taken into account is that the high cost of production and low value added in several public sector units is not necessarily because of management deficiencies but because of outdated technology, inappropriate location, non-marketable product mix and other extraneous factors. The government may still consider it appropriate to continue with investment in some public sector units for strategic or equity reasons (say, development of certain regions). However, it would be much better to select only those units for preservation which specifically satisfy the strategic or social objectives rather than further invest in public enterprises which are not generating adequate returns.

Similarly, while availability of capital is no longer a constraint to development in view of international capital mobility, any policy measure to liberalize foreign direct investment continues to attract political controversy in India. The suspicion with which investment is viewed is also a direct consequence of the colonial experience in the nineteenth century and the first half of the twentieth century. During that period, direct foreign investment conferred ownership and management rights on foreigners who exploited these rights to 'drain' investible surpluses and resources out of India. For this reason, the national political movement during the pre-independence period regarded foreign domination of Indian industry as a major cause of the country's poverty. While this was indeed the case fifty or sixty years ago, the situation today is vastly different. Indian industry and infrastructure are now largely owned by Indians. At the beginning of the twenty-first century, the share of foreign direct investment in the total capital stock in Indian industry is among the lowest in the world and relatively insignificant in relation to the size of the economy. In 2003–04, for example, foreign direct investment was only 0.7 per cent of the national income. Nevertheless, the same old attitudes continue to play a decisive role in determining the evolution of policy on foreign investment.

A much better approach would be to specify that for the next decade (or some such period), India would follow exactly the same policy as, say, China in respect of foreign direct investment. In other words, a foreign investor would have an equal choice of investing in India or China (or both). If, after the specified period, Indian markets were found to be flooded with foreign investment, and such investment formed a sizeable proportion of total capital formation (which was unlikely), then the policy could be reviewed. A concomitant of the above approach would, of course, be to ensure that Indian markets were competitive and open and not monopolistic with high levels of effective protection.

The hangover of the past is also reflected in the continuing dominant role of the bureaucracy in determining policy outcomes. A basic premise of India's Plans, as well as the early development literature, was that the required administrative response to fulfil the ambitious public investment targets and regulate the economy would be forthcoming in ample measure at different levels of administration—from the centre to the village level. The administration was expected to work in complete harmony to carry out the various tasks selflessly in the public interest. While most of the economy was still in private hands, a large bureaucracy was nurtured to regulate and control it. Thus, under India's early Plans, 'a burgeoning bureaucracy became the surrogate for socialism'.[6] By the early 1960s, when the Third Plan was launched, it had become clear that the expansion of administrative responsibilities was itself an important cause of inefficiency and delay. The Third Plan document was frank enough to observe that 'as large burdens are thrown on the administrative structure, it grows in size and as its size increases, it becomes slower in its functioning. Delays occur and affect operations at every stage and the expected outputs are further deferred.'[7]

Although the problem was recognized more than four decades ago, the proliferation of the bureaucracy has continued unabated and the administrative structure has become less and less functional despite significant liberalization of the economy in the 1990s. On all counts, the old bureaucratic and regulatory framework has become even more cumbersome. More and more agencies have been set up to regulate, control or oversee agencies set up earlier. A business environment survey carried out by the World Bank revealed that managers reported spending 5 per cent of their time dealing with government officials in Latin American countries, and about twice that in the transition economies of eastern Europe. In India, the average share of the time managers spent in dealing with the bureaucracy, even after the economic reforms of the 1990s, was 16 per cent.[8]

In addition to the regulatory control and several inspections imposed by federal agencies, there is a plethora of administrative rules and regulations imposed by state and local governments. These differ from state to state and from district to district within a state. Small and medium firms are the worst affected as they tend to have less developed political contacts for overcoming administrative barriers.

There are, of course, several important policy areas where there has been a welcome and decisive break from the past since 1991. These include the abolition of the industrial licensing system (with some exceptions), abolition of controls on capital issues, liberalization of the import licensing system, substantial lowering of tariffs on imports and adoption of a realistic exchange rate policy. Economic reforms in these areas have no doubt yielded positive results. The average trend rate of growth is now close to 6 per cent, the corporate private sector is showing signs of resurgence, access to domestic capital markets has become easy and, above all, the balance of payments and the reserves position have become strong. The point of drawing attention to certain other important areas where the deadweight of the past is holding back policy reforms is simply to highlight the fact that further acceleration of the growth rate and higher public investment in areas which benefit the poor (for example, public irrigation, rural infrastructure, literacy and health) are unlikely to occur until the old mindset changes. Unfortunately, from present indications, the probability of any positive action in the crucial areas mentioned above as well as certain other areas (such as labour reforms) remains very low.

The Power of Distributional Coalitions

At the time of independence, India's feudal past, large-scale poverty, vast differences in the distribution of income and wealth and its divided social structure created doubts whether its unity as a nation and its democratic experiment with adult franchise would last for very long. Some of these doubts were further reinforced by the violence during Partition and later the differences among the states over official languages and financial devolution. However, after India successfully went through three or four general elections, and the country's federal system became politically viable and generally accepted across the country, India's democratic experiment won worldwide admiration.

A number of theories have been advanced to explain the reasons for India's survival as a democracy despite its many internal contradictions. Several studies spread over the past forty years by scholars like Paul Brass, Myron Weiner, Francine Frankel, Lloyd and Susan Rudolph, Atul Kohli, Rajni Kothari and many others have tried to understand the reasons for this phenomenon. They have also provided alternative explanations as to why India's democracy has survived despite many conflicts, and its failure to deliver adequate economic benefits to its people. A useful survey of their findings may be found in a book by S.D. Sharma (2003).[9] The research findings and various hypotheses advanced by scholars are certainly useful in understanding the nature of India's democracy and the various forces at work in determining its evolution. However, in a functioning democracy like India's, where the vast majority of voters are poor, it is still difficult to understand why policies that do not benefit them continue to enjoy so much political support.

While there may be a number of alternative explanations for this state of affairs, perhaps the most convincing answer is to be found in the observed fact that, as highlighted in the public choice theory, the political decision-making process on economic issues in most democracies is driven by special interests rather than the common interests of the general public. These special interests also happen to be more diverse in India than in other, more mature, economies. There are special regional interests not only among the states, but also within states depending on the electoral strength of the party in power in different parts of the state. Economic policy-making at the political level is further affected by the occupational divide (for example, farm vs. non-farm), the size of the enterprise (for example, large vs. small), caste, religion, political affiliations of trade unions or the asset class of power-wielders, and a host of other divisive factors. As a result, most of the economic benefits of specific government decisions are likely to flow to a special interest group or, in Mancur Olson's famous phrase, to 'distributional coalitions'. These coalitions are always more interested in influencing the distribution of wealth and income in their favour rather than in the generation of additional output which has to be shared with the rest of society.

Also, the delivery of government benefits to special groups has given rise to a whole process of bargaining and conflict resolution among various interests. As a result, a large number of middlemen have emerged across the political spectrum. Further, as elections have become more expensive and more frequent with an uncertain time period during which funds can be collected in different states, there is greater tolerance of political corruption as an unavoidable feature of the electoral process.

Thus, contrary to what was envisaged by the founding fathers of our republic, and contrary to the vision of our planners, in several crucial areas the political–economic balance in actual practice has turned out to be narrow and wasteful. How did the stranglehold of special interests last so long; where were the majority of the people who did not gain sufficiently from the economic bargaining process? The answer is not difficult to find. The simple fact is that the so-called majority is fractured into a large number of subgroups of individuals who are divided among themselves by several factors (such as caste, religion, location or occupation), while special interests are united in protecting their share of the economic pie. This is really why the so-called 'haves' are so much more powerful than the 'have-nots' in our society. It is, for example, the trade unions of employed persons (or the 'haves') that are likely to go on strike when their economic interests are threatened, rather than the vast majority of the unemployed (or the 'have-nots') across the country.

At this point, I must make it clear that the important role of special interests in determining political economy outcomes is not an argument in favour of unfettered free markets, or the need for an economy without government regulations and laws. The issue here is not 'markets vs. government'. The problem with the Indian economy is not that its market is less or more free, but that its freedom is in the wrong domains. It is common knowledge that in most parts of India, government permissions, regulatory approvals or licences can be obtained at a price. In these domains, the problem is that of excessive marketization. On the other hand, in other areas where the market ought to be more free (for example, the labour market or international trade), India is strapped in bureaucratic red tape.

Two more caveats are necessary when considering the power of dominant coalitions in determining economic policy outcomes in our country. The point is not that these coalitions always emerge as winners in determining the direction of public policy, or that all politicians pander only to special interests. There are honourable exceptions, and there certainly are leaders who give primacy to the general interest; but they are likely to be exceptions rather than the rule. They are also likely to face considerable hurdles in successfully pursuing economic policies which adversely affect the special interests of the organized groups. Similarly, there are situations (such as war, natural catastrophes or religious conflicts) when a unity of purpose emerges among all sections of the people to promote the common good.

It is the power of special interests and dominant coalitions which explains why, in India, policies and programmes that benefit only a small proportion of the poor command such substantial support among all political parties. Thus, for example, the creation of additional government jobs at two or three times the market wage rates is the favourite preoccupation of most ministers in charge of administrative ministries and public enterprises. Over time, the expansion of the government's salary bill has fiscally disempowered most states (and the centre), leaving them with very little capacity to undertake capital expenditure to improve facilities and public services for the vast majority of the people. Yet, despite the huge fiscal drain, the number of government jobs in relation to the size of a state's population is relatively small and benefits only a handful of persons in the state capital. Their unions are also the most powerful in determining the government's expenditure priorities. The same is true of the passionate advocacy of job reservations for particular sections of the people. Only a very insignificant percentage of the population belonging to a particular reserved category is actually benefited, but the political noise about the benefit of such reservations for the disadvantaged and the poor is enormous. The point here is not whether reservations are desirable or not. There is undoubtedly a good case for them. However, it is striking that the dominant political coalitions seem to be more interested in the distribution of the few available jobs, rather than in increasing overall output, employment and the general welfare of the people.

It is no wonder then that even in those states that have a substantial proportion of the poor and the unemployed, the salaries of government servants, their pensions and interest on past loans exhaust more than 85 per cent of revenue receipts. The combined revenue deficit as a proportion of the total fiscal deficit of states shot up from 30 per cent in the first half of the 1990s to over 60 per cent by the end of the decade. A consequence of the fiscal squeeze in the states has been a sharp fall in the share of capital expenditure in total expenditure. Capital expenditure, which was already low (at only 20 per cent of state budgets in the late 1980s), further declined to less than 10 per cent in the late 1990s. Capital expenditure, particularly on roads and other infrastructure facilities, generally benefits people as a whole, while revenue expenditure (whose largest component is salaries) benefits only the fortunate few who have government jobs. People certainly have the political power to exercise their franchise and change the government, but increasingly the economy of the State works only in favour of the few who have the political power and their special constituencies.

An important area of the economy, which has been badly affected by fiscal disempowerment in the states in recent years, is that of agriculture. Since 1994–95, the rate of growth in agricultural production has been down to less than 2 per cent per year compared with over 4 per cent earlier (since 1980–81). With the exception of one or two years, monsoons have generally been good. However, the availability of public irrigation and power to the average farmer has deteriorated because of low investment, poor maintenance and administrative apathy. An important reason for this state of affairs is lack of financial resources with district authorities, including local panchayats, for capital investment or maintenance. The decline in the rate of growth in agriculture is a primary cause of high levels of poverty and increasing disparity in growth of incomes in sectors which are dependent on private investment and sectors which are dependent on public investment. The need to reduce subsidies which do not benefit the poor and increase public investment seldom figure in the public debate among political parties or political leaders even though areas with agriculture as the primary occupation send the largest number of representatives to Parliament and state legislatures.

The Disjuncture between Economics and Politics

In a recent essay, Pranab Bardhan has drawn attention to the growing disjuncture between economics and politics in India.[10] While democracy has clearly spread to the remotest area of the country in ever-widening circles of political awareness among hitherto subordinate groups, the political system has also become increasingly unresponsive to the economic interests of the median number of the poor disadvantaged groups. Politicians are seldom penalized by the electorate for their endemic poverty or the erosion of the public delivery system. There are now very few assurances that commitments made by one government (or leader) will be kept by successive ones, or even by itself under pressure. A political party that introduces some reforms (for example, disinvestment in privatization of public enterprises) is likely to be quick to oppose them when it is no longer in power.

Barring a few occasions when a particular issue acquires overwhelming national importance, such as the Emergency or India's role during the war in Bangladesh, there is also no discernible pattern which shows why particular parties or candidates win or lose elections. Until the elections in 1977 after the Emergency, the Congress party was returned to power, with varying majority, at the centre and in most of the states, irrespective of the economic results of the policies pursued by it. India had its first severe foreign exchange crisis in 1956, and it became increasingly dependent on official aid from abroad for more than thirty-five years after that. Yet a staple of the economic agenda put forward by the government and the Planning Commission over these years was a clarion call for 'self-reliance' and control over non-official foreign capital inflows. The removal of poverty through government control over investments and an expanding public sector were also important parts of the economic agenda. The anti-poverty objective found a particularly powerful expression in the slogan *Garibi Hatao* (Remove Poverty) during the 1971 elections. The government, which had already been in power for twenty-four years without being able to remove poverty, won the elections again with a massive majority on the basis of this promise! During all these years India also had one of the lowest growth rates in the developing world and the highest number of poor people.

The growth rate picked up after 1980, when the Congress party was returned to power after three years of a Janata Party government. However, it lost the elections again in 1989 for reasons which had little to do with the economy (although by that time an external crisis was brewing because of excess external borrowings and rising fiscal deficits). The Congress party came back to power again in

1991 in the midst of one of the worst economic crises, and launched a programme of economic reforms that was universally acclaimed. The crisis was soon over and India became externally strong. However, the party lost the next elections in 1996! The NDA—the National Democratic Alliance—government, which was voted out of power in 2004, by any reckoning also had a good economic record with strong external reserves, low inflation and high growth in 2003–04.

The chronicle clearly establishes the absence of economic performance as a factor in determining electoral outcomes. Economic considerations seem to be even less important at the state level. In the two largest states, Bihar and Uttar Pradesh, different parties with no credible record of economic performance or pro-poor policies have been returned to power time and again. As for individual members of Parliament, a report based on returns filed by candidates in the 2004 Lok Sabha elections shows that as many as one hundred members (in a House of 543 members) had criminal charges against them.[11] In addition to various other crimes (such as murder, fraud or kidnapping), almost all of these members had charges of financial corruption against them. Candidates with charge sheets against them belonged to all parties contesting the elections, and in small parties, the percentage of winning candidates against whom there where criminal charge sheets was 40 per cent or more. Six of these members are now ministers in the Union cabinet. The previous Lok Sabha also had a sizeable number of members who had criminal charges against them. Thus, the economic progress and success or failure in removing poverty have very little effect on electoral outcomes despite the overwhelming attention paid to these objectives in party manifestos and election campaigns.

It may be recalled that during the freedom struggle, an important unifying political force across the country was the desire to break away from the impact of colonial economic policies which had kept India poor and stagnant. In the post-independence period, for the first fifteen years or so, the Five Year Plans had raised high hopes of India becoming an economic and industrial power in the foreseeable future. In addition to his political charisma, Pandit Jawaharlal Nehru's initiative in launching India's ambitious Plans and the expectations they generated in all sections of the people was an important reason for the massive electoral mandates in favour of the Congress during the first three general elections after independence. However, after one of the worst droughts in 1965, it was becoming increasingly clear that India's development strategy and economic policies were not yielding the results and benefits claimed for them. While the electoral rhetoric still proclaimed the supreme importance of anti-poverty programmes and self-reliance, the economic record of the government in achieving these objectives became less and less important over time.

Against this background, a question that needs to be explored further is: If the economy ceased to be a unifying political force among the national electorate after 1965, was there any other national issue of equal importance which could have played a similar role in determining electoral outcomes? Two other national issues of abiding concern to all citizens of a country are, of course, foreign policy and defence. If something extraordinary happens in these areas, then naturally the government in office is likely to be affected, favourably or adversely, during the elections. For example, the Congress party's hold over the electorate was adversely affected after the Chinese incursion in 1962. On the other hand, the party gained immensely from India's successful intervention during the war in Bangladesh in 1971. However, such episodes are few and far between. In any case, there is not much difference in the political stance of different parties on issues relating to defence or foreign policy. In these areas there is a unity of purpose which cuts across party lines.

Apart from the economy, foreign policy and defence, there are generally no other national issues of similar importance which can play a dominant role in determining electoral outcomes across the country. It is not surprising, therefore, that gradually sectarian, local and regional issues have begun to play an increasing role in determining electoral outcomes. This explains the increasing importance of regional parties and the reason why the electoral verdict has become more divisive and fractured across the country. It has also changed the shape of the electoral agenda and the role of political parties and their leaders during elections.

Sectarian and local issues, when seen in the national context, naturally become more divisive. If there is a government of a different party or parties at the centre, the lack of development and continuing poverty in a particular state can always be said to be due to inadequate assistance from the centre. Similarly, there is much greater stress on reservations or the distribution of existing jobs, or the extension of special benefits to particular castes or particular sections of people, areas or occupations. The nature of the accountability of regional parties for performance in their states as well as of their leaders has also changed. They are not accountable for the failure to deliver what they promise or for the generation of employment or incomes for the poor, as some other party or some other centre of power can always be blamed for the continuing poverty and lack of progress.

At the centre, with the emergence of coalition governments of various shades with marked differences in ideologies and regional affiliations, accountability for actual performance has also tended to be weak. The expectation of a short tenure has added to the insensitivity of ministers to the long-term impact of the policies espoused by them. Fiscal accountability has become further and further removed, as a failure on the fiscal front can always be attributed to the actions of the previous government or to the unavoidable compulsions of coalition politics. Big promises for poverty alleviation or employment generation are made, but it is expected that a new government would have taken office by the time the actual results of these policies become evident. In addition to political apathy and lack of accountability for economic performance, there is the growing ineffectiveness of most institutions—courts, bureaucracies and police. According to Mehta (2003), 'They are so riddled with perverse incentive structures, that accountability is almost impossible. Most proposals for administrative reform simply add another layer of superintendence to existing institutions without seriously addressing the question of why so few in the state, honest or not, act to enhance the accountability of their institutions.'[12]

To conclude, there are several powerful forces at work, which may adversely affect India's economic performance in the future. The actual outcome may not be up to India's high potential unless there is a significant change in policy perceptions. There is increasing disjuncture between politics and economics, the power of special interests in determining policies of the state has increased, there is growing fiscal disempowerment, and governments are less accountable for the outcome of policies initiated by them. While the vigour and variety of India's democratic politics is a matter of comfort and joy, its lack of success in serving the real economic interests of the vast majority of the people, particularly the poor, is a matter of deep concern. At the beginning of the twenty-first century, after more than fifty years of development planning, India is also facing a growing crisis of governance. This is the subject of the next chapter.

References

1. Parikh, K. (1999), *Economy in India Briefing: A Transformative Fifty Years*, published by M.E. Sharp Inc., New York for Asia Society; Rosenweig, J.A. (1998), *Winning the Global Game*, The Free Press, New York.

2. Basu, K. (Ed.) (2004), *India's Emerging Economy: Performance and Prospects in the 1990s and Beyond*, Oxford University Press, New Delhi.

3. Jalan, Bimal (2002), 'India's Economy in the Twenty-first Century: A New Beginning or a False Dawn?' in *India's Economy in the New Millennium: Selected Essays*, UBS Publishers, Delhi.

4. Chandra, B. (1992), 'The Colonial Legacy', in Bimal Jalan (Ed.), *The Indian Economy: Problems and Prospects*, Penguin, New Delhi.

5. Acharya, S. (2004), 'Bad Ideas Vs. Good Men', *The Economic Times*, 22 January 2004; Panagariya, A. (2004), 'Goodbye to Double-digit Growth Rate', *The Economic Times*, 30 June 2004.

6. Basu, K. (Ed.), 2004, p.19.

7. *The Third Five Year Plan* (1961), Government of India, p.277.

8. *India: Reducing Poverty, Accelerating Development (2000)*, World Bank, Washington, D.C.

9. Sharma, S.D. (2004), *Development and Democracy in India*, Rawat Publications, New Delhi.

10. Bardhan, P. (2003), 'Disjuncture in the Indian Reform Process: Some Reflections', in K. Basu (Ed.), 2004. Also, see 'Political-economy and Governance Issues in the Indian Economic Reform Process', K.R. Narayanan Oration, Australian National University, Canberra, 2003.

11. *Outlook*, 12 June 2004, p.32.

12. Mehta, P.B. (2003), *The Burden of Democracy*, Penguin, New Delhi, p.132.

THREE

The Crisis of Governance

The crisis of governance in India, and the apathy of the governance structure towards the welfare of the general public, need no introduction. The observation of the high-level National Commission to Review the Working of the Constitution (Chairman: Justice M.N. Venkatachaliah) on the subject of governance speaks for itself:

> There is a fundamental breach of the constitutional faith on the part of Governments and their method of governance lies in the neglect of the people who are the ultimate source of all political authority. Public servants and institutions are not alive to the basic imperative that they are servants of the people meant to serve them. The dignity of the individual enshrined in the Constitution has remained an unredeemed pledge. There is, thus, a loss of faith in the governments and governance. Citizens see their governments besieged by uncontrollable events and are losing faith in institutions. Society is unable to cope with current events. (Venkatachaliah Commission 2002, p.50)

Lately, India has been in the news for its economic performance. It has also emerged as a leading exporter of software services and other high-technology exports. At the same time, despite its high growth potential, India also has the highest number of persons below the poverty line in the world. The estimates of the number of poor persons in India vary depending on the methodology used for estimation. However, even the most conservative estimates released by government agencies show that as many as 300 million Indians are below the poverty line, and do not earn enough to ensure even the minimum intake of food and nutrition. The conditions prevailing in its urban slums and rural areas are among the worst in the world, and even the most optimistic observers do not foresee any possibility of a dramatic improvement in the near future.

Over the years, the government has launched a large number of programmes which are 'targeted' to remove poverty through the creation of jobs, the provision of subsidized credit to the poor, or the delivery of free food in exchange for work. These programmes have no doubt benefited the poor, and helped to reduce the extent of poverty; however, all field studies as well as casual observation suggest that leakages in government-funded anti-poverty programmes are very high. In the late 1980s, leakages in these programmes were as high as 85 per cent, according to the then prime minister, Rajiv Gandhi.[1] Since then, the position is likely to have become worse rather than better because of political corruption and administrative ineptitude.

The urban–rural divide in the access to even the most essential public services, such as drinking water and sanitation, is striking. Thus, according to the National Sample Surveys, only 18.7 per cent of persons in rural areas (as compared with 70 per cent in urban areas) have access to piped water, which is the safest and easiest source of drinking water.[2]

The surveys have also found that in urban areas, the high-income households and not the poor households use the major share of subsidized water. Similarly, only 20 per cent of the rural households have access to sanitation facilities (as compared with 75 per cent of the urban households).

Ironically, a substantial part of the funds allocated for anti-poverty programmes in the annual budget also remains unutilized or is diverted by state governments and local authorities to meet other revenue expenditure. According to an expert commission set up by the Supreme Court of India (in response to a Public Interest Litigation), even Maharashtra, which has a well-established administration, failed to utilize as much as 78 per cent of the allocation of funds made by the centre for providing nutritious food to children as part of the prime minister's Gramin Yojana Scheme. Instead, it demanded funds from a large number of parents of poor children to fulfil the state's obligations. The position was worse in several other states, such as Bihar, Jharkhand and Uttaranchal, that were reviewed by the expert commission. In Jharkhand, for example, the government had failed to avail of the entire budget allocation 'because financial sanction could not be issued on time.'[3]

It is equally shocking that out of the relatively small budget expenditure on anti-poverty programmes, as much as 70 to 80 per cent is on account of the salaries of government servants at the various stages of implementation of these programmes (from the central ministries to the village level). The same is true of subsidized credit provided by the refinance agencies and banks owned by the central government. Thus, subsidized credit provided at 6 per cent per annum by the central refinancing agency has to pass through state, district and primary cooperative credit agencies before it reaches the farmer. The intermediation costs are more than double the initial interest rate of 6 per cent charged by the central agency, and the cost of credit to the farmer at the delivery point is 14 per cent or higher.

The Poor in 'Shining India'

The dichotomy between a 'shining', fast-growing India and its persistent poverty is certainly a puzzle which has baffled many development economists as well as ideologues. The answer to this puzzle does not lie in the proposition, advanced by some economists and central planners of the old school, that there is an inherent conflict between the objective of raising the rates of growth of the economy and that of reducing poverty. As it happens, the global experience is that countries and regions that have registered high and sustained rates of growth over a reasonable period of time are also the ones that have achieved the best results in reducing poverty and improving the health and nutrition of their people. In some cases, the progress in reducing poverty or improving the level of human development indicators has no doubt been much greater than would seem warranted by their rates of growth, as has happened in Kerala and Sri Lanka. There are also cases where high growth has been combined with a worsening of the poverty ratio, as in Brazil in the 1970s, or where high per capita incomes have not resulted in adequate progress in education and other social services, the situation in some oil-rich countries. However, such cases are not many and they have their own special reasons. It is also becoming evident that Sri Lanka and Kerala, which despite low growth made commendable progress in poverty alleviation, are now finding it difficult to sustain the process. Per capita expenditures on anti-poverty programmes have declined because of fiscal stringency. And with low industrial growth, unemployment has become a pervasive problem. This is a major obstacle to further progress on the poverty front.

It is obvious that poverty alleviation in a low-income country with poor basic amenities and poor availability of essential public services (such as primary education, water, power and transport) is feasible only if the government has the financial capacity to create the necessary infrastructure for the provision of such services to the poor. It is also likely that the higher the rate of growth of the economy, the higher is the growth of government revenues and its capacity to finance social expenditure likely to be. Whether the government actually does so or not is naturally a matter of public policy (Dreze and Sen 1989).[4] However, a low growth rate is not pro-poor. Nor does it help the debate on social or public policies. It is legitimate to ask for more government expenditure and more government intervention in favour of the poor or for more pro-employment growth policies. But it is fallacious to argue that the government can be more pro-poor in a stagnant or low-growth economy for any length of time.

As mentioned in the previous chapter, the real answer to the puzzle about India's high growth combined with persistent poverty lies in what can be perhaps described as the growing 'public–private' dichotomy in our economic life. It is a striking fact of our situation that economic renewal and positive growth impulses are occurring largely outside the public sector—at the level of private corporations (for example, software companies), autonomous institutions (for example, IIMs or IITs), or individuals at the top of their professions in India and abroad. In the governmental or public sector, on the other hand, we see a marked deterioration at all levels—not only in terms of output, profits and public savings, but also in the provision of vital public services in the fields of education, health, water and transport. These two elements—fiscal deterioration and the inability to provide essential services—are, of course, intimately connected. In India, most of the public resources are now dissipated in the payment of salaries or interest on debt with little or no resources available for the expansion of public or publicly supported services in vital sectors.

The widespread and persistent poverty, despite high growth in the private sector and some parts of the public sector (such as the oil companies, where the government has a relatively strong monopolistic position), can only be explained by the inability of the administrative structure, consisting of ministers and civil servants, to manage resources efficiently and deliver public services without massive leakages. Let us briefly look at the problems that bedevil our public delivery systems.

• We can be justifiably proud of the fact that the rule of law prevails in our country, and that even the mightiest are not above the law. The delays in the judicial process may be legendary, but there is widespread respect for the rule of law. However, for historical reasons, it is also a fact that our legal system provides full protection to the private interests of the so-called 'public servant', often at the expense of the public that he or she is supposed to serve. In addition to complete job security, any group of public servants in any public sector organization—hospitals, universities, schools, banks, buses, post offices, railways, municipalities—can go on strike in search of higher wages, promotions and bonuses for themselves, irrespective of the costs and inconvenience to the public (in whose name they have been appointed in the first place). There is little or no accountability of the public servant for non-performance of duty. This is despite a Supreme Court judgement in 2003 against strike by government servants as no penal provisions have yet been prescribed by the government.

• The 'authority' of governments, both at the centre and in the states, to enforce their decisions has eroded over time. Governments can pass orders, for example, for the relocation of unauthorized industrial units or other structures, but implementation can be delayed if they run counter to the private interests of some (at the expense of the general interest). Similarly, governments may decide to restructure public utilities to cut down waste or output losses, but these decisions do not necessarily have to be implemented if they adversely affect the interests of public servants employed in these organizations.

• Governments at different levels may announce plans and programmes to provide social services (such as expanding literacy), but these initiatives are unlikely to be implemented on the grounds of fiscal stringency. For example, in 1994, the Tenth Finance Commission projected a rate of growth in real terms of 2.5 per cent for expenditure on elementary education up to the end of the century for four states where the incidence of poverty and illiteracy was among the highest in the country. This projected rate of growth in expenditure was lower than the growth of the population in the relevant age group, and grossly insufficient to cover new programmes for adult illiterates. In the ten years since the commission's report, it is interesting to note that the real expenditure on elementary education, outside of salaries of government teachers, in these four states has actually been negative!

• The processes and procedures for conducting business in government and public service organizations, over time, have become non-functional. There are multiple departments involved in the simplest of decisions, and administrative rules generally concentrate on the process rather than the results. There is very little decentralization of decision-making powers, particularly financial powers. Thus, while local authorities have been given significant authority in some states to implement national programmes, their financial authority is limited. Transfers to local authorities for health spending, for example, average less than 15 per cent of state government budgets.

• The multiplicity of functions and responsibilities placed upon ill-equipped and ill-trained staff in public offices and local institutions makes it almost impossible to deliver services with any degree of efficiency, particularly in rural areas. For example, a 'multipurpose' female health worker is required to perform as many as forty-seven tasks, to be undertaken on a regular basis!

To improve governance and provide better services to the public within a democratic framework, it is now necessary to impose greater accountability on both ministers and civil servants. Some of the essential elements of reform are discussed below.

The Myth of Collective Responsibility

Each department and ministry of the government is headed by a politically appointed minister, who is a member of Parliament and represents the party in power (which has a majority in Parliament either on its own or as a part of a coalition government). The minister is the chief executive of the ministry, and reports to the prime minister. In a parliamentary form of government, the cabinet is supposed to have a collective responsibility for all the decisions taken by each ministry either on its own or with the approval of the cabinet. Each minister, as a member of the cabinet, is also answerable to Parliament. Members of Parliament have the right to ask questions, move call attention motions, introduce resolutions and demand accountability for all the decisions taken by ministers and the performance of their ministries.

In a country like India, with one of the lowest per capita income levels in the world and the highest number of poor persons who also have the right to vote, alleviation of poverty, creation of employment opportunities and provision of better public services to the poor are among the principal items on the economic agenda of every political party at the time of elections. The instrumentalities and specific policies proposed to be adopted if voted to power may vary from one party to another, but the anti-poverty objective is the same. In view of this, it is surprising that despite the increasing frequency of elections and the different combinations of parties that have formed governments in the last fifteen years, the public delivery system has continued to deteriorate. While there have been numerous questions, calling attention motions and resolutions in Parliament on unemployment and the non-availability of basic infrastructure in rural areas, no minister has actually been held accountable (or censured) for the poor performance of his or her ministry in these vital areas.

The reason for parliamentary inertia and the non-accountability of ministers for the performance of their ministries lies in the supremacy of the parties and their leaders in the political system. As long as the party or the combination of parties has a majority in Parliament, ministers are supreme because they enjoy the patronage of the leader of the party or the prime minister. No resolution or calling attention motion can be adopted in Parliament without majority support, and no harm can come to the minister or his special interests or political constituency if his party is in the majority. The position becomes worse in a coalition government with a thin majority and the disparate ideologies of constituent parties. In this case, ministers belonging to a party other than that of the prime minister are not even accountable to him or to the cabinet formed by him. In the past fifteen years, there have been a number of governments (including the government which came to office after the general elections in 2004) where the cabinet has been headed by a party with less than one-third of the total number of seats in the Lok Sabha. The survival of the government thus depends crucially on the continued support of other parties, large and small, local and national. It is not surprising, therefore, that the concept of ministerial responsibility for the performance of ministries or the government as a whole has become largely illusory.

The fractured electoral verdict in the 2004 Lok Sabha polls—with no national party securing even one-third of the seats and the emergence of a large number of local parties as pre-election allies—only reinforces the scenario. The government will no doubt continue to have some excellent ministers with a deep commitment to the public good. However, on the whole, the sense of collective responsibility and accountability for the management of public resources and delivery of services to the poor is likely to be absent. This ground reality can no longer be denied.

Assuming that political parties, the civil society and the enlightened members of the Indian public are serious about removing the worst forms of poverty and deprivation, then a new institutional initiative is urgently required to enforce ministerial responsibility for the efficient delivery of public services and anti-poverty programmes all over the country. This can be achieved only if the cherished doctrine of 'collective' responsibility for all actions of the government is replaced by the notion of 'individual' responsibility of ministers for implementing programmes that are of direct concern to the poor. The doctrine of collective responsibility can continue to prevail for all other political purposes, including the continuation of a government in office.

In practice, as mentioned above, the notion of the 'collective responsibility' of the cabinet has already more or less disappeared in coalition governments, with different parties pulling in different directions. A recent example of the arbitrary exercise of power by a minister in office, which would have had a long-term impact on the quality of management education, was the decision announced by his ministry in March 2004 to drastically reduce the financial autonomy enjoyed by the Indian Institutes of Management (IIMs). This decision was made by the minister without any reference to or endorsement of the cabinet. After the change of government in May 2004, the new minister decided to reverse the decision without having to consult the cabinet. The decision of the new minister has been widely welcomed by the IIMs, and is certainly in the country's interest. The episode shows that the exercise of enormous powers available to ministries has now become the individual responsibility of ministers even in cases of long-term importance for the future of the country. If 'powers' can be exercised without collective responsibility, then there is an equally strong case for ministers to take individual responsibility for their 'duties' in certain vital areas, like poverty alleviation.

The objective of better delivery of public services can be achieved if quantitative annual targets are agreed upon with each of the concerned ministries at the time of the annual budget and each minister is made responsible to Parliament for achieving those targets. Quantitative annual targets are already being worked out as part of the annual plans of ministries, but they have no sanctity or force of ministerial responsibility behind them. These targets are primarily for obtaining higher budgetary allocations, and for claiming credit for larger and larger Plans. There is no accountability for the actual implementation or achievement of agreed targets. In future, the Planning Commission should also be made responsible for placing before Parliament a report on actual achievements in relation to the agreed targets. This report should be the focal point of discussion in Parliament on a ministry's budget, and if there is a shortfall of more than the agreed percentage (say, 15 or 20 per cent), then the minister must be held responsible, and expected to relinquish ministerial office for at least one year. If there is a change of ministers during the course of the year, then the new minister must once again affirm or change the target with the approval of Parliament.

One obstacle in assigning individual ministerial responsibility for realizing public service targets is that a number of other ministries, in addition to the administrative ministry, is involved in actual implementation and approval of budgetary expenditure. Thus the Planning Commission and the Public Investment Board may be involved in project appraisal and approval of investment programmes. The Ministry of Finance may be involved in approval of actual expenditure, even if the necessary expenditure is already included in the budget. Yet another ministry may be involved in the design of a particular programme if that programme also cuts across its area of administrative responsibility. It may, therefore, be considered unreasonable to hold a particular minister responsible for failure to realize the announced public service targets as the reasons for non-performance may lie elsewhere. Under the present system, where there is substantial diffusion and overlapping of administrative responsibility, there is certainly merit in this argument. However, the answer to this problem lies in reforming the administrative system rather than in denying individual ministerial responsibility for implementation of an approved programme. Henceforth, it may be stipulated that all concerned ministries, including the ministries of finance and planning, would be appropriately consulted at the time of fixing the annual target rather than at the stage of implementation. If necessary budgetary resources are not available or the design of the programme is not yet approved, the announcement of the anti-poverty and other targets should also be deferred. Once the target is announced by a ministry, it should have the full authority to implement it and it would be the only ministry which is held accountable for actual performance.

The proposal is certainly unconventional and contrary to established parliamentary practice, which does not recognize individual ministerial responsibility for a ministry's performance. However, this is the only feasible option if the country is serious about reversing the deterioration of public services due to financial leakages and ministerial apathy. It would be desirable if, with the full support of all the parties in the government and the opposition, a binding resolution to this effect is adopted by Parliament as early as possible. A higher degree of direct ministerial responsibility for performance, along with a restructuring of the administrative system (see below) is now essential if India is to succeed in abolishing the worst forms of poverty by, say, 2020.

The Failure of Administration

The actual delivery of public services is obviously dependent on government officers and employees who occupy administrative positions at different layers of the hierarchy in the delivery process. There are senior officials in various ministries at the centre who are responsible for deciding the policy, the amount of budgetary grant or loan to be made available to state governments and the implementing agency responsible for carrying out the project. At the state or agency level, there are officials in the main secretariat or elsewhere who have to disburse the funds and take various other administrative decisions. Then there are district-level officials who are responsible for monitoring the progress of the programme, making site visits and filing returns. Finally there are ground staff at the primary level who are actually responsible for delivering a particular service to the public, removing deficiencies, attending to complaints and levying a token fee, if necessary. If there is a problem or deficiency at the field level (say, the non-availability of medicines or lack of funds), it is likely to be referred to the district, state or central level, or all three, for resolution. In most cases, particularly those involving staff or funds, officials in multiple agencies at all three levels are likely to be involved.

A great deal has been written on the atrophy, non-accountability, corruption and ineptitude of the Indian civil services (Ray 2001).[5] In addition to academics, outside observers, international agencies and the general public, a number of civil servants have also written their memoirs or recounted their experiences after their retirement from the highest offices of the State. There is now almost complete unanimity that, despite having some of the best and the brightest persons in the civil services, the system as a whole has become non-functional, and there is very little possibility of reforming it. The situation has arisen despite a lot of trying, including efforts made at different levels by distinguished committees, commissions, associations and public-spirited persons. These efforts have come to naught because the system is dominated by internal conflicts of interest (for example, powerful but separate trade unions for different classes of government employees), political interference, statutory provisions, complicated seniority-bound procedures, fiscal stringency and the proliferation of agencies which operate at cross purposes without any clear division of work. Thus a highly reputed civil servant, who became the administrative head of the Ministry of Finance in 1961, found that 'in a matter of days, my worst fears of ossification of the bureaucratic system were proved right', and that this system by its own momentum had become 'so complicated that it became a veritable jungle' (Bhoothalingam 1993, p.104).[6]

This was the state of affairs in 1961, only fourteen years after India became independent. Since independence, the numbers in the bureaucracy have increased ten times in the central government alone (from about 0.4 million to over 4 million), and fiscal costs have increased by more than 100 times, but the administrative system has become worse year after year.

India's civil services are now also overburdened by an imbalance in the skill mix. Nearly 93 per cent of the civil service is comprised of the so-called Class III and Class IV employees in the Government of India. The percentage of such employees in state governments is even higher. They include frontline delivery workers, but the overwhelming numbers are clerks, typists, messengers, peons and sweepers. The overabundance of support personnel often exists alongside chronic shortages of skilled staff in essential services, such as water supply, health, sanitation and schools. To make matters worse, the civil service is divided into dozens of cadres, each with its own terms and conditions of service, with controlling authorities widely dispersed among various departments. Some staff, particularly senior staff, are transferred after short tenures (ranging from a few days to less than a year), but other staff cannot be transferred between departments or locations irrespective of functional requirements.

The administrative cobweb, with multiple agencies and no clear-cut demarcation of functions, creates insuperable problems and delays for all those who have to deal with a government agency for any purpose, large or small. According to a survey, at least six or more central ministries are involved in controlling or regulating every sector of the economy.[7] Thus, matters concerning the food processing industry normally have to go through nine ministries—agriculture, food and consumer affairs, health, commerce, food processing, rural development and others. The Ministry of Human Resource Development (HRD) at the centre (which was earlier called the Ministry of Education) now consists of four separate departments: the Department of Education, the Department of Culture, the Department of Women and Child Development, and the Department of Youth Affairs and Sports. Each of these departments has several sub-departments or divisions. The Department of

Education has separate units concerned with primary education, secondary education, technical education, teachers' education, higher education, book promotion and copyright, planning, languages and Sanskrit, district education and international relations, among others. Similarly, the Department of Women and Child Development and the separate Department of Youth Affairs and Sports have several divisions concerned with different aspects. All these departments have several commissions and subsidiary organization under them reporting to different divisions and authorities with cross-cutting functions. While there is multiplicity of specialized departments, divisions and organization, none of them has adequate authority to take any decision concerning even the most non-controversial items. Take, for example, the matter of providing better sports facilities for young women in schools. A proposal to this effect would require consideration by practically all the divisions and organizations as it concerns women, sports, education, youth and, perhaps, welfare! After the matter has gone around the ministry's various units (with conflicting views and objectives) over several months or years, it would need to be considered by an inter-departmental committee of the ministry, then a number of secretaries, and finally the minister, all of whom are likely to have the most casual acquaintance with the subject. Thereafter, of course, if finance, law, planning, security and any other aspects are also involved, the matter would need to be referred to other ministries with their own multiple layers of departments and divisions.

Administrative staff strength is large in every department, but in view of its Byzantine structure, it cannot be used productively. In Uttar Pradesh, for example, the Public Works Department has a total strength of 77,000. With fifty-one full-time workers for every 100 kilometres of road, it has one of the highest manual staffing ratios in India.[8]

Wages paid to road workers are three times as high as the market wage rate. However, because of high absenteeism, absence of work culture and lack of supervision and equipment, the roads in the state are among the worst in India.

The burden of weak administration naturally falls mainly on the poor because of the indifference of government staff to them. A survey by the Public Affairs Centre found that, in Delhi, the average slum dweller needed to make six trips to a government agency to resolve a problem, and in only 6 per cent of the cases was his or her problem attended to. Other households had to make four trips, and in their case the rate of success was substantially higher, but still only 27 per cent.[9]

The insensitivity of the administrative system to the needs of the poor, even to prevent starvation, has been confirmed by first-hand surveys and reports by journalists and non-governmental organizations. One such survey revealed that in remote villages, children were dying of hunger despite the country's godowns bursting at the seams with public stocks of food and despite more than Rs. 40,000 crores that the central government had allocated for expenditure on anti-poverty schemes. On further investigation, it was found that 'the vast network of officials set up take care of the interests of the poor was in denial'.[10] Similarly, it was found that many villages were without water even after rains because water channels and tanks had fallen into disuse as the government had announced its intention to provide piped water out of taps. While some construction work had been started to provide tap water, the project was left unfinished. The villagers had access to neither tap water nor old-style tanks or wells within a reasonable distance.

This is a long litany of woes. It is important to understand the complexity of the present system, its historical evolution, and its past failures to work out a possible solution. So far, the effort has largely been confined to reforming the system from within by issuing circulars for expeditious delivery, decentralization of some functions to panchayats (without delegation of financial powers), creating new specialized departments (with existing staff skills), and greater monitoring. In addition, some effort has also been made to make the system more accountable by providing the public with the right to seek information and easier access to credit for self-help groups and micro-credit organizations. As a result of these initiatives, in some states, there has been some improvement in the delivery system. There are also some organizations of the government (for example, the Department of Space, the Telecom Department, the National Highway Authority and Delhi Metro) which despite all the staff handicaps have achieved excellent results.

However, these are exceptions—welcome as they are—to the general rule of administrative decay in the functioning of the government. With the emergence of coalition governments of disparate groups and parties, the administrative structure is likely to continue as it is, or deteriorate further, rather than show any improvement. As in the past, there will be individual persons at high political or administrative levels with integrity and commitment to the public good. However, given the dominance of special interests in the political parties as well as the civil services, it is unlikely that the administrative system can be improved from within. A reformist minister with a successful record in the erstwhile government has thus observed that

> Ministers are ill equipped. Secretaries know the intricacies much better—but they are so thoroughly domesticated by the system that they do not have the passion which alone would sustain effort for long enough to effect real change ... With but a toothpick of jurisdiction and authority in the hands of each, and that too for fleeting intervals, how

can one ensure massive, across the board, simultaneous sustained effort? (Arun Shourie 2004)[11]

Shourie has suggested that, while efforts to make the system more accountable must continue, it is not feasible to reform from within, and that the only solution is to reduce the role of the government by removing a particular function from its jurisdiction. He has cited the example of the reform of the licensing system in telecom. Earlier, these licences were service-specific, user-specific, technology-specific, area-specific and vintage-specific. This wide differentiation in the types of licences required constant state intervention to remove the difficulties faced by operators and consumers. It also led to inefficient services, and widespread corrupt practices by suppliers as well as supervisors. This unwieldy system was replaced, after a great deal of effort, by a universal access licence which was made freely available at a pre-announced fee. This reform has reduced the role and functions of the State, and has also improved services to the consumers. Thus, according to Shourie, 'the real way out of the maze is not reforming some particular procedure but redefining the nature of the State itself'.

This is sage advice, based on experience, and deserves to be followed in all sectors of the economy. In addition, it is also necessary to make a distinction between policy direction (that is, laying down policy guidelines and monitoring performance), and the actual implementation of programmes. In addition to lack of adequate resources, the most important problem in the public delivery system is the mismanagement and theft of the available facilities and resources. For example, in respect of as essential a service as drinking water, distribution and transmission losses are estimated to be 40 to 50 per cent. The same is true of electricity supply to rural areas in most states. If transmission and distribution losses were reduced by even half through better management of the available capacity, the improvement in the supply of services and financial savings would be immense.

International experience in the management of public services shows that the objective can be achieved if a distinction is made between the ownership of these services (by the government) and the delivery of such services (by private and local enterprises). A compilation of twenty-four case studies from twelve countries all over the world has concluded that in every case where the management of a public service was contracted out to private enterprises, the distribution and quality of the service improved and the net cost to the public was reduced.[12] What is more, a large number of jobs and many new enterprises were also created. In most cases, the public authorities retained the responsibility for regulating and monitoring the activities, providing subsidies where necessary and laying down distribution guidelines. In India, two noteworthy examples of public–private collaboration in the area of public services are the public call offices (PCOs), which revolutionalized the availability of telephone services all over the country in the 1990s, and the Sulabh Sauchalayas, which are estimated to have provided sanitation facilities to ten million people at very low cost.

In several countries, the model of public–private partnership (or 'micro-privatization' under public supervision) has replaced the old system of public ownership and public delivery in certain important sectors. In India, in respect of telephones as well as sanitation services, the new initiatives were supplemental to the public sector facilities. In other words, they did not replace the public sector organizations responsible for the delivery of these services. In view of entrenched political and bureaucratic interests as well as for practical reasons (to avoid the disruption of existing public sector services), this was a wise decision. The supplemental approach expanded the availability of services and created a more competitive environment without affecting government employees and raising resistance. It is now necessary to adopt a similar approach in respect of all essential public services. No new facilities or employees should be added in the public sector, and additional budgetary allocations (over and above the existing salary and maintenance expenditures) at the centre, states and local levels should be made for the delivery of services by private enterprises, including non-government professional organizations.

In addition to the need for improving the administrative system for delivery of public services, there is the larger question of the reform of the entire civil service apparatus for better governance of the country. A reference was made to the observations of a distinguished civil servant, S. Bhoothalingam, as early as 1961 about the 'ossification of the bureaucratic system'. Similar observations were made in the Third Five Year Plan, which was launched in the same year. Since then, a number of other distinguished civil servants have expressed the same sentiments. While a host of recommendations have been made by numerous high-powered committees to improve the system, the general view among experts and experienced civil servants now seems to that the reform of the system is not feasible. This is not because the country does not know what to do but because of political resistance to reform of the civil service. Thus a former cabinet secretary, who has also recently written his memoirs, has pointed out that:

> Politics having become the most lucrative business in the country, with few checks and controls, there is a compulsion for the minister or political leader to attempt to coerce civil servants to collude with him for mutual benefit ... The service rules and procedure have been progressively adapted to facilitate this process. (Subramaniam 2004)[13]

In view of the past failures in reforming the civil service, it is also now increasingly believed that the suggestions for reforming the bureaucracy are really meant to divert attention from the real causes of administrative decay. Thus, in the words of a former finance secretary to the Government of India:

> Over the last two decades, a system has evolved in which the politician uses the threat of transfer, tempts the bureaucrat with lucrative posting and exploits the desperation of senior officers for post retirement sinecures. Senior officers align themselves informally while in service and formally after retirement with one political party or another ... It is futile to expect radical suggestions for reform from committees comprising civil servants or outside 'experts'. A committee is a cul-de-sac into which ideas are lured and then quietly strangled. (Kumar 2004)[14]

Considering the widespread cynicism about political willingness to effect civil service reforms, it is perhaps best for me not to waste too much time or space to go over this question once again. However, the issue is too important to be completely ignored. Based on personal observations, I would like to highlight a few points before concluding this chapter.

As citizens, whether we like it or not, we need an efficient civil service. It is, therefore, of the utmost importance that a civil society movement is launched for reform of the civil service without delay. Several non-governmental organizations have already done good work in this area (such as Common Cause headed by H.D. Shourie), but much more needs to be done. The issue needs as much attention as is given to several other vital issues of public concern, such as freedom of speech, gender equality, reservation of seats for representation of women in legislatures, and so on. There is political resistance by governments for reform in all these areas. However, with popular support, India has been able to make at least some progress even on the most contentious issues. The question of civil service reform and better governance should now figure high on the public agenda.

The most critical issue which needs to be tackled is the 'motivational' or morale issue at the higher levels of civil services. Civil servants, who join government service through a competitive process, are generally highly competent and motivated when they enter the service. However, after a few years of service, there is a perceptible decline in morale, commitment and efficiency. An important reason for this decline is the power available to politicians in power to harass a civil servant who does not abide by their wishes. The easiest method of doing so, which is now widely used by ministers, is to frequently transfer civil servants at very short notice. After a few such transfers, cynicism sets in as most civil servants would rather abide by ministerial wishes than put themselves and their families through the inconvenience caused by yet another transfer. Civil servants at higher levels, who technically pass the orders of transfers, are also reluctant to intervene. With greater political instability over the last fifteen years, since 1989, a pernicious development has been that transfer decisions of even lower level officials, which used to be taken earlier by the civil service itself, are now taken by ministers (Alexander 2004).[15] The common belief in the civil service is that in order to survive, ministers and their officers (however corrupt or incompetent) must be kept in good humour.

In order to improve the morale of the civil service, the ministerial powers to transfer civil servants without adequate cause need to be moderated as early as possible. Except at the highest levels, say the first two rungs of the service (secretary and additional secretary), who have to deal directly with ministers, the powers of posting and transfers should be entirely within the jurisdiction of the civil service. An appropriate mechanism (such as the public services boards) is already in place, and they should be given full and final powers for posting of civil servants up to the designated level. For the highest levels in the service, postings and transfers may continue to be subject to the approval of the political authority. However, once a civil servant has been appointed to a particular post with due approval of the government, his or her further transfer by the same government before a stipulated period (of, say, three years) should be effected only for non-performance or lack of integrity. The reasons should be stated in writing in specific terms with appropriate documentation justifying the decision, rather than left vague. The officer should have access to the reasons for transfer and should have the right to appeal to a designated higher authority.

A further measure for greater empowerment of civil service is to reform the procedure for launching vigilance inquiries and the number of agencies involved in such investigations. This matter is dealt with at greater length in the next chapter. The ease with which investigations can be launched without adequate cause, and then closed after several years for lack of evidence, is a major cause of harassment and pain for the honest civil servant. Increasingly, there is a tendency among civil servants at higher levels to avoid taking a decision, according to the rules in place, on a financial or a controversial matter without seeking ministerial approval. In case a decision on such a matter is taken by the civil servant (who is otherwise competent or authorized to do so), it is feared that an inquiry may be launched at the instance of a minister or a business group which is adversely affected by that decision. The fear of taking decisions is a major cause of delays and atrophy in the decision-making process.

The basic issue that needs to be tackled for improving the morale of the civil service is really that of 'separation of powers' *within* the executive—between ministers and civil servants in so far as posting, transfers, promotions and other similar administrative matters are concerned. The separation of powers among three branches of government— the executive, the legislature and the judiciary—is already enshrined in the Constitution. Although there has been considerable encroachment of the executive powers into legislative, and even judicial areas, it can still be said that these three separate branches enjoy a certain measure of autonomy and independence (if they wish to exercise it). *Within* the executive branch, however, the civil service is now completely dependent on the pleasure of the ministers in regard to even the most mundane and routine administrative matters. It is essential to revert to a rule-based system of administration, which circumscribes the powers of politicians and confers greater authority on the civil service itself for self-regulation.

The greater empowerment of the civil service must, of course, go hand in hand with greater accountability of civil servants for their performance and ethical conduct. While, within the executive branch, the civil service has lost power, so far as the public is concerned, it is still the most powerful agency of the state. By all accounts, for various reasons India has now acquired the unenviable distinction of having one of the most corrupt civil services in the world, particularly in its dealings with the average citizen. The civil service corruption (in addition to political corruption) is also the root cause of lower productivity in the use of resources and the fiscal disempowerment of the State. The economic effects of corruption, and the strategy for reducing the supply and demand of corruption in India, form the subject of the next chapter. This chapter also deals with certain measures which are necessary for making the civil service more accountable and less arbitrary in its actions.

References

1. Gandhi, R. (1989), cited in *India Today*, 30 November 1989, p.16.

2. Ratna Reddy, V. (2001), 'Declining Social Consumption in India', *Economic and Political Weekly*, 21 July 2001.

3. *The Times of India*, 17 September 2004, Mumbai, p.9.

4. Dreze, Jean and Sen, A.K. (1989), *Hunger and Public Action*, Oxford University Press, New Delhi.

5. Ray, J.K. (2001), *India: In Search of Good Governance*, K.K. Bagchi & Company, Calcutta.

6. Bhoothalingam, S. (1993), *Reflections on An Era: Memoirs of a Civil Servant*, Affiliated East-West Press, New Delhi.

7. *The Times of India*, 2 June 2004, p.17.

8. World Bank (2003), *India: Sustaining Reform, Reducing Poverty*, Oxford University Press, Delhi, p.39.

9. Shekhar, S. and Balakrishnan, S. (1999), *Voices from the Capital: A Report Card on Public Service in Delhi*, Public Affairs Centre, Bangalore.

10. Singh, T. (2004), 'Fifth Column', *The Indian Express*, 19 September 2004, p.7.

11. Shourie, A. (2004), *Governance: Things to Do*, New Delhi (mimeo).

12. Harper, M. (2000), *Public Services through Private Enterprises*, Vistaar Publications, New Delhi.

13. Subramaniam, T.S.R. (2004), 'All the Netaji's Men', *The Indian Express*, 17 September 2004, p.9.

14. Kumar, A. (2004), 'Chasing a Will o' the Wisp?', *The Indian Express*, 25 September 2004, p.8.

15. Alexander, P.C. (2004), *Through the Corridors of Power*, HarperCollins, New Delhi.

FOUR

The Supply and Demand of Corruption

The most repugnant aspect of corruption in India is not that it is there, nor that it is so pervasive, but that it is widely accepted as an unavoidable feature of Indian life. Corruption, in one form or another, has been present in all societies from time immemorial. Two thousand years ago, it was Kautilya who first discussed it at some length in his *Arthashastra*.[1] However, while its presence was recognized, corruption was generally regarded as being morally and ethically reprehensible. In more recent years, this view of corruption seems to have undergone a slow, imperceptible but definite change. There is now much greater tolerance of corruption as an essential element of India's democracy and its governance structure.

At the political level, corruption among parties and politicians is believed to be unavoidable as elections have become expensive and funds have to be raised, by whatever means, to contest them. Similarly, in defence of the high incidence of bureaucratic corruption, it is argued that civil servants in India are not paid well or that such corruption is a 'universal phenomenon'. The Indian defence of a corrupt bureaucracy nowadays is similar to the one that used to be offered in Uganda in the 1980s, when Uganda was regarded as one of the most openly corrupt countries in the world. It was argued that 'the civil servant had either to survive by lowering his standard of ethics, performance and dutifulness or remain upright and perish. He chose to survive!' (Lindaner and Nunberg 1994).[2] Corporates in India, large and small, also choose to survive and thrive by participating actively in corruption on the grounds that it is the only way to get their business done. Interestingly, corruption in businesses in India is perhaps as internal (that is, between a private buyer and a private seller or financier) as it is external (that is, between a private firm and the government). The common man or woman also has to participate in corruption because there is simply no other option if he or she has to get a ration card, a licence, a permission or a registration.

In addition to its wide acceptance as a necessary evil, another area of grave concern is the interlocking or 'vertical integration' of corruption at various levels of the government hierarchy—elected politicians, higher bureaucracy and lower bureaucracy (Guhan and Paul 1997).[3] The normal assumption that the principals at each of the higher levels would be committed to ensure that their subordinates would act according to probity is no longer valid. In a situation in which principals and agents collude with each other in corruption, the problem of tackling it has become much more intractable. Along with vertical integration of corruption at various levels of the executive branch, there is also horizontal spread of corruption to other public institutions, including legislatures, parts of judiciary, media as well as independent professions. This has made the prevention and control of corruption even more difficult. As if all this were not enough, another unfortunate development has been the politicization of corruption. Increasingly, cases of corruption are being given a political colour without any serious intent to tackle the problem. This has facilitated the entry into politics of persons with a track record of corruption. The public no longer knows whom to trust—the accuser or the accused.

Corruption is a major hurdle in growth, development and poverty alleviation. Research has established that corruption reduces productivity, lowers investment, causes fiscal drain and has a debilitating effect on efficiency. These adverse effects of corruption are not generally recognized by India's political and legal institutions or its public. This chapter aims to bring together the available information on the ill effects of corruption on public welfare and the country's economic potential. A related purpose is to suggest measures that can reduce the extent of corruption, and its widespread social acceptance, by eliminating the causes that give rise to it. Both the demand and the supply of corruption need to be reduced by redefining the role of the State and improving its governance structure.

The Economic Effects of Corruption

Until recently, the economic effects of corruption were seldom discussed in the literature on development economics. The reason for this neglect was partly respect for the sovereignty of newly independent developing countries, and partly because of the difficulty of defining and measuring corruption in a statistically relevant way. In the last few years, however, there has been an explosion of interest among researchers in empirical and quantitative analysis of the effects of corruption on investment, growth and public finances. Most of this research has originated in international financial institutions, particularly the World Bank and the International Monetary Fund. These institutions have been involved in financing development and structural adjustment programmes in developing countries over the last five decades or more. These programmes seldom yielded the kind of positive economic results that were initially expected. Over time, it became apparent that part of the reason was the high incidence of corruption. Important findings of the latest research on corruption are available in an IMF publication by Abed and Gupta (2002).[4] Investment choices are often driven by their potential for corruption and illicit gains rather than their contribution to national output or the real rate of return on projects. In addition to a strong political bias in favour of launching unproductive and high cost projects in uneconomic locations, there is also an inherent bias against spending on 'operation and maintenance' and on human capital formation. These activities generally have lower scope for illegitimate monetary transfers to intermediaries (Tanzi and Davoodi 2002).[5]

An important finding of recent empirical research is that corruption has a significant negative impact on the ratio of investment to national income, and that an improvement in the corruption index (that is, reduction in corruption) can significantly increase the investment ratio and enhance growth. According to Mauro (1955), in a country where corruption is widespread, a reduction in corruption by, say, 50 per cent, can increase the growth rate by nearly 1.5 percentage points.[6] While no independent estimate has been made for the growth-reducing effects of governmental and private corruption in India, my rough calculations, based on Mauro's econometric model and anecdotal evidence, is that it could be even higher—nearly two percentage points or so. In other words, all things remaining the same, if there were no corruption, India's growth rate would have been nearly 8 per cent per annum in the 1980s and 1990s, rather than close to 6 per cent.

The reason why corruption has such debilitating effects on investment and growth is not only the illegal and clandestine transfer of funds from one set of persons to another, but also the economic effects of corruption on investment choice. Thus, high corruption is often associated with the wrong choice of public projects and project delays, leading to low productivity and low fiscal revenues, low maintenance expenditure and low quality of essential public infrastructure which, in turn, increases the cost of production of goods and services by business enterprises.[7]

This phenomenon and the negative circular relationship between corruption and investment explain the 'poverty trap' in which many low-income countries, including India, find themselves. This also presents an important dilemma for public policy and development strategy. In countries with poor infrastructure, particularly in rural areas with high incidence of poverty, public investment is the essential instrument through which productivity and income levels can be raised. At the same time, the higher the level of public investment in relation to GDP, the higher is likely to be the level of corruption and its negative effects on growth. The solution thus becomes the problem. The only way in which this conundrum can be resolved is to take administrative measures to break the nexus between investment and corruption.

Another interesting finding of empirical research is that the adverse economic effect of corruption is more pronounced on small enterprises and the overall growth of employment in the economy. Thus, a survey of 3000 enterprises across twenty transition economies, covering all regions, found that corruption and anti-competitive practices were perceived as the most difficult obstacles by start-up firms (EBRD 1999).[8] For large enterprises, corruption often increases profits as it allows them to enjoy monopoly rents and scale economies. For small enterprises, it raises costs and reduces profits because they have to make payments that do not contribute to productivity or output but are necessary for their survival. In order to avoid undue harassment, bribes, which may amount to a substantial portion of the operating costs of such enterprises, have to be paid to meet the demands of a host of inspectors working in concert with each other. This becomes an important cause of sickness of small industries requiring further assistance from local governments or banks, which in turn affects their viability.

Since independence, in addition to giving various incentives to promote small enterprises, central and state governments have also launched a variety of anti-poverty rural development and special employment programmes (such as the Food for Work Programme) to directly benefit the poor and the disadvantaged. Most of the benefits of these programmes are also appropriated by bureaucrats and middlemen at various levels of the administrative hierarchy. Thus, in a memorable and widely quoted observation, after visiting some of these programmes Prime Minister Rajiv Gandhi had pointed out that 'out of Rs. 100 crore allocated to an anti-poverty project, I know that only Rs. 15 crore reaches the people. The remainder is gobbled up by middlemen, power brokers, contractors and the corrupt.'[9]

In fact, the poor are the worst affected by widespread corruption in delivery of health and other essential public services. In order to enhance the scope for corruption, government expenditures are inflated and wasteful projects and programmes are taken up, including purchase of spurious drugs and unsafe equipment causing hazards to safety, life and longevity. While the better-off have access to private providers of essential services, the poor have to necessarily rely on public agencies. They are, however, unable to pay bribes in order to obtain even the minimum benefits to which they are entitled. Thus, another economic effect of corruption is that it further aggravates inequality in an already unequal society.

As is well known, in order to improve the public delivery of essential services to the poor, India implemented a countrywide experiment with decentralization to local governments after the passage of the 73rd and 74th

Constitutional Amendments in the early 1990s. While the scale and scope of this reform is impressive, research in the actual working of the decentralized system in different states has revealed wide disparity.[10] In most states, only a limited extent of autonomy has been awarded to panchayats. In particular, education and health, two vital services for the poor, remain entirely outside the province of panchayati authority. There is almost no devolution of unconditional grants to gram panchayats. The only authority devolved to panchayats concerns the selection of local beneficiaries of government programmes, and management and implementation of local infrastructure projects covering roads, irrigation and housing. As the fund allocation at the district level is grossly insufficient to cover all eligible beneficiaries, corruption and political favouritism at the panchayat level in some states have become routine. This has further accentuated inequality even among the relatively poorer sections of the village population. Kerala is among the few states where levels of citizen participation in local decision making on the use of public resources for health and education are significant, and where the level of corruption in the distribution of benefits to the poor is relatively low.[11]

Corruption is also an important cause of fiscal drain and higher inflation in developing societies. There is strong evidence that countries with high levels of corruption tend to have lower collection of tax revenues in relation to their national incomes (Friedman et al. 2000).[12] Corruption also has a statistically significant negative correlation with receipts from personal income taxes since private negotiation with tax inspectors is a common practice in many developing countries, including India. It is estimated that a one-point increase in corruption is associated with as much as a 0.63 per cent decline in receipts from individual income taxes. Indirect tax collections, particularly revenue from customs duties and excise duties, are also highly sensitive to the degree of corruption. It has also been found that the higher the level of duties, and the greater the variability in tax rates (depending on the type of goods), the higher will be the scope for corruption and accompanying revenue drain. As rates increase and corruption rises, the tax system as a whole becomes less progressive.

In addition to rise in fiscal deficit and lower progressivity of the tax system, the quality of government expenditure also suffers. The selection of investment programmes, including anti-poverty projects, tends to be guided more by scope for graft and potential supply of corruption rather than their intrinsic costs and benefits. While elaborate procedures have been set up for tendering and open bidding, much of the mischief is done at the time of specifying the technical details of projects or programmes, which are so drafted as to ensure that the preferred contractors and suppliers are put at an advantage. For these as well as other reasons (particularly, the preponderance of non-productive revenue expenditure), a high fiscal deficit does not necessarily lead to higher investment or higher output. Despite persistent and high fiscal deficits over the past two decades, capital formation in the public sector in India has been low and declining with adverse effects on growth.

Thus, taken as a whole, contrary to popular perception, corruption is a major cause of economic backwardness, low growth, high incidence of poverty and fiscal crisis in developing countries. Further, according to surveys, the corruption perception index is also higher in countries that have lived longer under a central planning system, have a lower per capita income, and have made slow progress on structural reforms (Abed and Davoodi 2002).[13] These variables alone account for 86 per cent of the variation in corruption rankings for a sample of countries. Not surprisingly, India ranks high on all three variables as well as on the index of corruption.

The facts about the extent of corruption, and its pernicious effects on the delivery of public services, particularly to the vast majority of the poor, are known to governments as well as to the permanent civil service and the judiciary. Governments in office have periodically announced their intention to simplify procedures, improve delegation of powers and reduce corruption. Various measures have also been announced to improve the vigilance machinery and strengthen penal action against corrupt public officials. Unfortunately, over time, despite introduction of various anti-corruption measures, the administrative system has become more corruption-inducing rather than the other way round! Thus, in the words of a former home secretary to the Government of India, 'the government, in public perception, continues to be as corrupt as ever, if not more. Several decisions of the government in major fields such as power, petroleum, banking, disinvestments of shares of public sector undertakings, telecommunications and foreign investment have lacked consistency or rationale. The economic administration has reached new levels of imperviousness and disdain for public accountability and transparency.'[14]

There cannot be a more severe indictment of the prevailing situation by an insider who would have witnessed the working of the administrative system at close quarters. Let us now turn to possible approaches to tackle the problem, or at least reduce its further spread.

In India, the concern about administrative corruption is as old as the founding of our democratic republic. More than forty years ago, an important national committee on the prevention of corruption, the Santhanam Committee (1964), submitted a comprehensive report.[15] Since then, a number of other committees have been set up for the reform of the governance and administrative structure. Various other agencies including the Comptroller and Auditor General

(CAG), the Central Vigilance Commission (CVC), the Central Bureau of Investigation (CBI) and the Pay Commission have also submitted countless reports expressing their anguish over rising corruption and suggesting measures to combat it. Unfortunately, most of the actions taken by the various governments over the last forty years to launch new programmes have had the effect of increasing both the demand and the supply of corruption rather than reducing them. A number of new agencies are involved in preventing, investigating or punishing corruption with no effective results. Every ministry and agency involved in the delivery of programmes, government approvals and providing public services, now has vigilance departments and vigilance officers. To provide checks on arbitrary or personalized decision making, a large number of checkpoints have been set up which every file and every financial decision have to cross— both horizontally and vertically. Unfortunately, as a result, procedures have become long-winded and complex, and delays in decision-making processes have become legendary. The demand for and the supply of so-called 'speed money' (a socially accepted euphemism for bribes) has increased. In some ministries or agencies, where the top political leadership is also corrupt and powerful, the entire bureaucracy becomes an instrument for the extraction of bribes or rents from their clients. It also acquires a stake in protecting corruption and increasing its proceeds (Johnston 1997).[16]

An effective anti-corruption strategy would need to focus on institutional reform as well as effective measures which reduce both the 'demand' and the 'supply' of corruption. There are multiple investigating and prosecution agencies at the centre and in the states to fight corruption and convict the guilty. Yet the legal provisions and judicial processes are so cumbersome that cases of successful prosecution of corrupt civil servants or politicians are negligible. Institutional reform to reduce the number of agencies involved in the anti-corruption drive along with legal reform is now essential to provide swift and deterrent punishment to the corrupt. The supply side of the corruption equation can only be checked if there is a sizeable reduction in the size and functions of the government, and greater accountability of public servants for the discharge of their duties. Penalties for corruption, including dismissal from service, have to be swift so that they have a deterrent effect on the entire civil service and reduce incentives for corrupt behaviour. On the demand side, it is necessary to provide access to scarce public services, occupation and resources through transparent, non-discretionary procedures and market-related mechanisms. Similarly, administrative regulations and documentation requirements have to be substantially scaled down. Measures for institutional reform as well as the supply side and demand side anti-corruption measures are discussed below.

The Need for Institutional Reform

Corruption in India is now so entrenched that a serving member of India's administrative service (Das 2001)[17] has observed that:

> The corruption network in India is so perfectly orchestrated that there is a thriving internal economy linking principals and agents. The principals (ruling politicians) provide the opportunity and protection, while the agents (civil servants) pay for their spoils by sharing the bribe ... All the actors involved—ministers, civil servants, anti-corruption functionaries—have a stake in protecting corruption and increasing its proceeds, and also, in freezing out the critics of corruption. (pp.193–194)

While the number of agencies involved in collecting information, conducting searches and taking the necessary action to bring civil servants and politicians to book have multiplied over time, the quantity of corruption as well as the impunity with which it can be carried out has also expanded. The judiciary has passed severe edicts against the executive authority in corruption cases, but in most cases of importance, the investigation either remains incomplete or the evidence is weak. According to data collected by Das (2001), on cases referred to the CBI, the premier anti-corruption agency, the number of senior civil servants who have been punished for corruption or have lost their employment as a result of its investigations is negligible. In a few cases, where punishment has been awarded, the penalty has been relatively weak, with the result that the necessary deterrence is non-existent. The record of other central and state agencies is equally dismal if not worse. As for the powers of the judiciary and its role in anti-corruption cases, the following observation of Justice J.S. Verma (2004), a former Chief Justice of India, is noteworthy:

> The monitoring by the Supreme Court in the (Jain) Hawala case provided full autonomy to the CBI in the conduct of investigations by it, with the authority to prosecute all those found guilty by it. In spite of this freedom, the level of its performance can be gauged from the fact that charge sheets filed did not make out a prima facie case to frame the charge in any case, and all the accused were discharged by the court. The impression is that the purpose of filing half-baked charge sheets was only to get rid of the monitoring by the Supreme Court led by me.[18]

There are multiple causes for the relative ineffectiveness of India's judicial system in checking the incidence of corruption or disposal of even the most outrageous cases of corruption. These have been analysed in considerable detail by a number of committees, including the High Court Arrears Committees of 1949, 1972 and 1990, as well as several Law Commission reports. However, despite much soul-searching, debate and recommendations emanating from these high-level committees, the position in disposal of cases has become progressively worse. According to the Malimath Committee report, between 1968 and 1989, the number of pending cases multiplied almost four-fold.[19] The multiple levels of appeals available to the accused also ensures that a powerful person, particularly with a political background, can remain free for even two decades or more.

A welcome initiative has recently been taken by F.S. Nariman, member of Parliament, in introducing the Judicial Statistics Bill alongwith the Constitution (Amendment) Bill in the Rajya Sabha. The Bill aims at creation of authorities for judicial statistics at national, state and district levels. These authorities are expected to collect statistics about the cases, appeals, petitions and other matters filed in courts and other tribunals. The information collected by them will include the legal nature of the dispute, outcome of the dispute, number of hours taken in disposal of the cases, number of adjournments granted and the interval between filing of cases and their final disposal. Such statistical data will obviously be invaluable for determining action that needs to be taken for effecting improvements in expeditious hearing of cases, appeals, petitions and other matters. Availability of relevant statistics is the minimum requirement for speeding up the judicial system. It is hoped that Mr Nariman's proposal will be adopted as early as possible.

A proposal to set up a new authority, the Lokpal, which would have the power to investigate abuse of political power by ministers (including the prime minister) has also been under consideration for several years. However, if the experience of a similar agency at the state level, namely the Lokayukta, is any guide, the new agency will also fail miserably in providing any deterrence to political corruption. The record of the Delhi Lokayukta set up in December 2002, for example, has been dismal. As many as thirty-nine out of forty-four complaints filed against MLAs and ministers could not even be taken up for consideration, and no penal action has been taken in the remaining five cases because of legal infirmities and lack of investigating staff (*Indian Express*, 15 May 2004, p.1).

An essential component of an anti-corruption strategy for the future is to reduce and revamp the number of agencies and institutions involved in the investigation and prosecution of corruption cases. In any case, no new agency should be set up for this purpose. At the centre, as well as at state level, there should be only one specialized agency for the investigation and prosecution of large-value corruption cases against public servants, political representatives and ministers. The cases referred to it should be of significant importance in terms of value or national security or criminal conduct (such as fraud and smuggling). No more than a handful of major cases should be referred to it, and it should have sufficient access to funds and technical expertise to launch prosecution within ninety days of receiving a major complaint. The objective should be to provide deterrence and exemplary punishment in a few cases rather than try and tackle a multitude of cases, which cannot be done effectively. All other cases of corruption should be handled departmentally through an established and transparent procedure with the help of outside specialized and non-governmental investigative agencies.

It is possible that there are better solutions to correct the institutional mess. The important point is to create a new, simpler and effective procedure that will inflict heavy and deterrent punishment in at least a few corruption cases so that an example is set for the rest of the civil service.

Supply-side Measures

First and foremost, on the supply side, measures have to be taken to reduce the protection provided to government servants and other public servants under the Constitution and various judicial pronouncements. Most of the constitutional and statutory provisions were intended to provide reasonable security of tenure to civil servants, avoid arbitrary penal action, and ensure that 'due process' is followed in processing specific cases. However, the legal framework has become non-functional and has been effectively used to provide protection to organized corruption in government and public sector enterprises. A large number of cases have been filed in the courts after multiple levels of departmental inquiries lasting years, but to no avail. Even in the most outrageous cases (such as those involving high fiscal authorities like the chairman of Excise and Customs, who is responsible for realizing tax revenues amounting to more than Rs. 1,75,000 crore from custom duties on imports, excise duties on domestic output and other indirect taxes), the culprits are apprehended and sent to judicial custody for a few days. Thereafter, more often than not, they are released on bail and enjoy complete freedom of action, including the right to contest elections. During the period of suspension from service, which itself is a difficult and a long-drawn-out process, they are likely to enjoy the full benefits of government pay and perquisites. If there is sufficient evidence warranting dismissal from service, the necessary court orders—after several appeals—usually come through only after the official has retired from service!

Two statutory provisions, among several others, which deserve to be amended forthwith are: Article 311 of the Constitution of India, and the Official Secrets Act (1923). Originally, Article 311 of the Constitution was intended to provide constitutional safeguards for a person holding a 'civil post from being reduced in rank, removed or dismissed from service'. These safeguards were supposed to apply only to government servants—those directly employed by the government at the centre or in the states under any of the services. They were not supposed to apply to other 'public servants' employed by public sector enterprises or parastatal organizations. However, subsequent judicial pronouncements, for all practical purposes, have removed the distinction between civil servants and other public sector employees. This was done through an expansive interpretation of Articles 14 and 16 of the Constitution which incorporate the principle of 'natural justice' as a Fundamental Right of the people of India. Elaborate rules and procedures have been laid down under the provisions of Articles 14, 16 and 311 for inquiry, investigation and prosecution of all persons employed, directly or indirectly, fully or partially by the government (Pal 1999).[20] These rules ensure that even with the best will in the world, corrupt officials even with known disproportionate assets cannot be successfully prosecuted within a reasonable period of time.

The best way to remove the protection of law for corrupt government officials, and thereby reduce the supply of corruption, would be to remove from the purview of Article 311 all those who are charged with corrupt practices. The Fifth Pay Commission (1997) had made a similar though weaker recommendation:

> Government could take legal advice as to whether the provisions of Article 311 can be diluted with reference to employees who have either been caught red-handed under the Prevention of Corruption Act or who have been found after due investigation to be in possession of assets disproportionate to their known sources of income. In such cases, suspension could be mandatory. (Vol.1, p.210)

Even this recommendation has not been implemented. It would be appropriate if Article 311 is now amended to specifically provide that those who fulfil the conditions identified by the Fifth Pay Commission will not enjoy the benefit of this Article. The protection of the law available to such persons would be the same as that available to ordinary citizens of India under relevant laws. This will be fair and equitable.

The Indian Official Secrets Act, which was passed more than eighty years ago, in 1923, continues to be in force even today with some minor amendments. The provisions of this Act are so comprehensive that almost all information of the government can qualify to be classified as an official secret. Interestingly, nowhere have the words 'secret' or 'official secret' been defined precisely in the Act, and any kind of information can attract prosecution under the provisions of the Act, whatever the purpose or the impact. This Act and its wide ambit have provided comprehensive opportunities to officials and ministers to cover up their decisions to increase the supply of corruption, in addition to denying the people the benefit of vital information on government activities. Decisions can be taken which are contrary to facts as contained in the relevant files, judicial pronouncements, business rules or previous decisions of interest to the public. The secrecy surrounding the reasons for decisions taken, particularly decisions which have financial implications, makes it difficult, if not impossible, that cases of manifest corruption would be detected in time. The incentive for corrupt practices, in secrecy, has increased substantially with increase in political instability at the centre and in several states.

The 1923 Official Secrets Act deserves to be withdrawn as early as possible. In its place, a new Act may be passed which should incorporate a precise definition of what is considered secret, and which should confine the scope of secrecy to matters of national security and market-sensitive financial information. Matters which may be considered as being security-related or market-sensitive may also be defined precisely and confined to as few in number as possible. It may also be required that before a file is marked secret, a designated high official of the ministry should certify the reasons for doing so. In view of entrenched bureaucratic and political interests, a reform of the secrecy Act is not going to be easy. However, if the supply of corruption has to be curbed, this can no longer be avoided.

Another vital area which requires immediate legislative action is State-funding of political parties. The matter has been discussed from time to time, but no consensus has emerged. An equitable formula for the allocation of budgetary funds among different political parties is intrinsically difficult, particularly in a multiple-party democracy like India. As many as fifty-five recognized parties, in addition to independents and unrecognized parties, contested the 2004 Lok Sabha elections. If State funds were allocated to different parties according to the existing number of members of a party in Parliament or the legislatures, the parties in opposition would have found themselves at a disadvantage. On the other hand, if funds were allocated equally among, say, two or three major parties, then smaller parties would have been at a disadvantage.

Notwithstanding this difficulty, a solution to the problem faced by parties for financing elections has to be found. This is perhaps the most important reason why political corruption (even for disguised private gain) has acquired moral legitimacy. Based on the experience of countries where political funding of parties for elections has been instituted, a combination of the following three elements may provide a workable allocation formula.

• One of the highest elements of costs for parties during elections is television and newspaper advertising. The government should allocate a reasonable budget to cover advertising costs on public and private television and in newspapers for a specified time, over two or three weeks prior to the elections. The time allocated for the purpose should be reasonable so that different parties are able to communicate their message to the public effectively. The time allocation may be equal for parties which have, say, more than 15 per cent of the seats, and proportionately less for smaller parties. An equal distribution of time among the major parties for this purpose is fair as no party should enjoy a disproportionate advantage in conveying its message to the public. As part of this package, no party (or for that matter, government in office) should be permitted to undertake any additional television advertising. There could be a more liberal approach for advertising by parties in newspapers in local Indian languages.

• Similarly, reasonable transport costs by air and train for national parties with 15 per cent of the seats (and proportionately less for small parties) should be reimbursed by the government on the production of relevant bills for three or four weeks prior to the date of elections. Parties should be free to incur additional costs for travel, subject to any rules that may be laid down by the Election Commission. A similar approach can be adopted for the reimbursement of actual expenses for posters and other similar essential election expenditure.

• The reimbursement of actual expenditure for the above purposes, according to the rules laid down by the Election Commission, is likely to cover a substantial part of the legitimate electoral expenses of parties. In addition, a relatively small monetary allocation can be made to cover other expenditure (on staff and miscellaneous items). The allocation of budget funds to meet residual expenditure should, however, be weighted by the number of seats held by each party. The weights should be suitably devised to ensure that the larger the party, the higher is its entitlement for funds, but that the smaller parties are not put at an undue disadvantage.

The above is by no means a perfect formula, but it is fair and reasonable. It may be argued that the budget provisions required to cover the election costs would be high and would increase the fiscal deficit. While this is true, the increase in the overall percentage of the fiscal deficit as a proportion of GDP is unlikely to be very significant. In any case, considering its positive effect in reducing the supply of corruption, expenditure incurred on this account would be more than justified.

An alternative or supplemental approach is also feasible to reduce the fiscal cost of election-funding by the State. In order to meet the expenditure on this account, it would be desirable if the amounts presently allocated for the Member of Parliament Local Area Development Scheme (the MPLAD Scheme), and the outstanding unspent balance under this head, is diverted for this purpose. If this suggestion is accepted, no additional budgetary funds may in fact be required for election funding.

A related measure to diminish the supply of political corruption is to reduce the immense powers available to ministers in the decision-making process of a government in office. The fact that ministers are politically responsible to Parliament/legislatures has led to a situation where practically all decisions, including bureaucratic appointments and postings, require ministerial approval. Policy decisions on economic issues, and rules framed under them, are also so devised as to require a case-by-case approval. There is no reason why the postings of permanent civil servants, other than those on the personal staff of ministers, should require ministerial approval. Approval by civil service boards, as per the rules already in place, should be more than sufficient for this purpose. Similarly, while economic policy decisions can be taken by the cabinet or ministers, specific cases should invariably be decided by permanent administrative committees. They will, of course, be accountable to political authorities and, through them, to Parliament for decisions taken by them.

In countries with low corruption levels, transparency in the decision-making process and full disclosure of decisions taken in financial matters are the most powerful forms of ensuring accountability. Along with the abolition of the Official Secrets Act, it should be made mandatory for all ministers and departments of the government to make information on the decisions taken by them available to the public, particularly on matters that have financial implications (excluding purely administrative or security-related subjects). The information should be released frequently after allowing for a time lag where market-sensitive decisions are concerned. It may be clarified that information should be released by the ministries themselves without the need for any member of the public to ask for it. India is fortunate in that it has a free and vibrant media and strong civil society organizations (including non-governmental organizations, business associations, academia and think tanks). The free media and civil society institutions will constitute an effective deterrent to corruption, provided information on decisions taken by the government is available.

There is one important area where the supply of corruption creates its own demand. If administrative rules and regulations are complex and involve multiple agencies acting at cross purposes, then the public has no option but to purchase the required permits, licences and registrations by paying bribes. India's administrative system is probably among the most cumbersome in the world, where the public is completely at the mercy of the civil service for getting even the most ordinary permissions (such as a driving licence or the registration of land/real estate). Some measures which are necessary to reduce the demand for corruption are considered below.

Demand-side Measures

The demand for corruption has two components. The most pervasive and 'retail' component consists of the demand generated by members of the public who require various kinds of permissions or licences which are necessary to carry on with the ordinary business of life. Surveys done by the Public Affairs Centre in India some years ago have provided telling statistics about the extent of retail corruption in India. According to these surveys, every fourth person in one of the large cities in India ends up paying a bribe when dealing with agencies such as those for urban development, electricity, municipal services and telephone (Paul 1997).[21] In another large city, it is commonly believed that every person who has to deal with the income-tax department or any other tax agency has to pay a bribe even to get confirmation that tax has actually been paid!

The other component of the demand for corruption is the 'wholesale' component, which is selective and generated by a few corporates (including some large business houses) to take advantage of a restrictive practice or price control for their own pecuniary benefit. This component was most conspicuous during the industrial licensing and control era, when there were numerous controls on output, distribution and pricing. A well-known example of such comprehensive controls pertains to iron and steel in the 1960s and 1970s. As pointed out by S. Bhoothalingam (1993),[22] these controls were so detailed that every stage of production and movement of all categories of steel was subject to inspection by the relevant government agency. Prices at each stage of the transactions from the factory to the retail point were prescribed by the government. An unintended consequence of this system of controls was a proliferation in the demand for corruption by all producers, traders and consumers of steel at various stages (for example, for the procurement, movement or pricing of a particular consignment). A similar system prevailed in all imports and foreign exchange transactions. With the liberalization of the economy and the abolition of various kinds of licensing and pricing controls in the 1990s, the demand for wholesale corruption of this kind has reduced, but is not yet eliminated. There is still a long way to go.

While the policies for licensing, price controls, imports and distribution have been liberalized in the 1990s, the number of clearances required for setting up industrial plants and agencies involved in giving such clearances have in fact increased. The demand for 'wholesale' corruption, despite economic reforms, therefore continues to be strong. Thus, for example, in order to set up a medium-sized industrial factory, at least fifteen clearances from the state government and six or seven clearances from the central government are likely to be required. If coal or other inputs, which are under the control of both state and central governments, are required, then the project becomes even more complicated. Among some of the approvals required at the state level are: site clearance, land acquisition, fire safety, environmental impact assessment and consent, forest clearance, rehabilitation and resettlement plan, power connection, water, consent for road connection to the plant, mining clearance, and so on. In addition, central government approval is also likely to be required for environment, mining, fuel linkage, forest conservation, railway dispatches and conformity with safety or quality standards specified by the central bureaus or ministries. Many of these clearances are certainly necessary in the public interest; however, the main responsibility for providing such clearances is generally entrusted to non-professionals. The rules are highly complicated and often internally inconsistent. Each clearance is also likely to involve more than one government agency and several departments. To expedite clearances or overcome legitimate objections, corruption becomes unavoidable and is considered a necessary component of doing business in India.

After the reform process was initiated in the 1980s, and accelerated in the 1990s, there has been considerable debate in the country on the economic merits and demerits of liberalization and the reduction in the role of the State in the allocation of capital. Much of this debate has been in terms of an optimal or theoretically valid paradigm and ideology. Is liberalization theoretically superior to government intervention or is it not? Is globalization consistent with national sovereignty or is it not? Is reform of the public sector consistent with our socialist ideals or is it not? And so on. This debate misses an important reason for the growth-retarding effects of excessive State intervention— that it increases the incidence of corruption in the economic life of the country. Liberalization of production, distribution and pricing of goods and services, in addition to its positive effects on output, is also growth enhancing because of the reduction in the demand for corruption, provided policy liberalization is accompanied by procedural simplification and reduction in the number of clearances required and agencies involved in certifying adherence to multiple legal requirements.

Redefining the role of the State, simplification of administrative procedures and creating a more competitive environment in the economy are essential elements of the strategy for reducing the demand for corruption. However, it must be emphasized that the need to redefine the role of the State in the context of economic reforms does not mean a lesser role for the government or for public policy in widening opportunities and creating a positive environment for equitable development. In developing countries such as India, with massive illiteracy and underdevelopment of infrastructure, the government must continue to have a crucial role in creating the necessary conditions for growth through investments in areas such as education, health, water supply, irrigation and infrastructure. These tasks cannot be taken over by the market. Successful economic reforms must result in strengthening the ability of governments to do what they need to do by helping to generate higher growth, higher revenue and higher productivity.

The most urgent need for administrative reforms is in the areas of taxation and the provision of the services that affect the public directly. Tax rules and filing requirements have to be simple, non-discretionary and understandable to the taxpayers. This applies to central and state taxes as well as the various kinds of municipal taxes, including property tax. While tax papers and documents must be scrutinized by the relevant department, personal visits and searches by inspectors must be discontinued altogether (except in cases involving national security, organized crime, systemic fraud and smuggling). Such powers available to tax officials have added substantially to the demand for corruption by taxpayers in order to avoid harassment. The rate of conviction in search and seizure cases is insignificant.

Another disconcerting and surprising finding of research on income tax enforcement in India is that, despite enormous powers available under the law, the government has progressively diluted its prosecution effort away from powerful large-scale tax evaders towards small-scale evaders and those committing technical violations. Thus, out of thirteen successful prosecution cases decided for income tax violations in 1990, only three involved concealment of income; all others involved technical violations, such as failure to deposit tax deducted at source. No case involved an amount exceeding Rs. 50,000; and most of the offences were committed between ten and twenty-five years ago. The fraction of prosecution complaints that pertained to cases of tax evasion was approximately 100 per cent in the early 1970s, one-third in the late 1970s, dropping to less than one-tenth in the late 1980s. The rates of successful conviction have also dropped from around 70 per cent of cases in the early 1970s to between 20 and 30 per cent in the late 1980s. These are dismal statistics and provide powerful evidence of the ineffective exercise of discretion available to tax authorities.[23]

A simple and reasonable tax system, which is non-discretionary, is likely to be more effective in increasing revenues than the present system. An example is the reform of property taxation by the Municipal Corporation of Delhi (effective April 2004). The Unit Area Method, based on objective criteria (such as the size of the built-up area, location and date of construction) has replaced the old discretionary system where the rate depended on valuation by tax officials and inspectors. The new system has been the subject of criticism and protest by taxpayers as well as officials, but according to initial reports, tax collections had already shown an increase, and corruption had practically vanished.[24] Unfortunately, after a couple of months of good revenue collections, the state government decided to provide various exemptions from levy of property tax, which has adversely affected collections. However, this was due to a conscious political decision of the government unrelated to incidence of corruption. There is also an apocryphal story that when octroi checks were abolished by a state, the entire staff of the department went on a prolonged strike. Nevertheless, tax collections increased significantly because of voluntary tax compliance! Similar root and branch reforms are now essential in the entire tax system of India, from the central to the local level.

The system of providing various kinds of licences, registration and identification numbers to the general public should also be decentralized and 'outsourced' to different non-government companies/agencies on contract. An example of such 'outsourcing' in an otherwise routine matter is the issue of Permanent Account Numbers (PAN) to the Unit Trust of India by the Income Tax Department, which had accumulated a huge backlog of applications. As a result of this outsourcing, taxpayers now have quicker and easier access to this essential service. Since the outsourcing and decentralization of such services are likely to be distributed among a large number of organizations, subject to accountability and public satisfaction, there will be a significant reduction in the scope for corrupt practices. It may be emphasized that these kinds of reforms can be introduced without causing any harm to the interests of the staff of the relevant departments. They should be given security of their existing tenures, and a generous optional early retirement scheme should be made available to them. Surplus staff can be usefully employed in other parts of the concerned organization. However, even if they remain idle, the benefits to the public and the government as a whole are likely to far outweigh the costs.

There is no doubt that an effective anti-corruption strategy covering institutional reform as well as the supply and demand sides will substantially improve governance and the public delivery system in India. The resulting public confidence and trust in the government, its political leadership and administration, will also strengthen democracy. A by-product of a reduction in corruption due to economic reforms and the redefining of the role of the State in the economy will be to enhance the growth rate, productivity and revenues of the government. These, in turn, will enable and empower the government to improve public investment in important sectors, such as infrastructure and primary education.

References

1. Tanzi, V. (1998), 'Corruption Around the World: Causes, Consequences, Scope and Cures', *IMF Staff Papers*, vol. 45, December 1998.

2. Lindaner, D. and Nunberg, B. (Eds) (1994), *Rehabilitating Government: Pay and Employment Reform in Africa*, World Bank, Washington, D.C., p.27.

3. Guhan, S. and Paul, S. (1997), *Corruption in India: Agenda for Action*, Vision Books, Delhi.

4. Abed, G.T. and Gupta, S. (Eds) (2002), *Governance, Corruption and Economic Performance*, International Monetary Fund, Washington, D.C.

5. Tanzi, V. and Davoodi, H.R. (2002), 'Corruption, Public Investment, and Growth', in Abed and Gupta (Eds), 2002.

6. Mauro, P., 'Corruption and Growth', *Quarterly Journal of Economics*, August 1995.

7. Tanzi, V. and Davoodi, H.R., 'Corruption, Public Investment, and Growth', in Abed and Gupta (Eds), 2002.

8. European Bank for Reconstruction and Development (1999), *Ten Years of Transition*, London.

9. Gandhi, R. (1989), cited in *India Today*, 30 November 1989, p.16.

10. Mookherjee, D. (2004), *The Crisis in Government Accountability*, Oxford University Press, New Delhi.

11. Mathew, G. and Nayak, R. (1996), 'Panchayats at Work', *Economic and Political Weekly*, 6 June 1996.

12. Friedman, E. and others (2000), 'Dodging the Grabbing Hand: The Determinants of Unofficial Activity in 69 Countries', *Journal of Public Economics*, vol. 76.

13. Abed, G.T. and Davoodi, H.R. (2002), 'Corruption, Structural Reforms, and Economic Performance', in Abed and Gupta (Eds), 2002.

14. Godbole, M. (1997), 'Corruption, Public Interference and the Civil Service' in Guhan and Paul, 1997.

15. Report of the Committee on Prevention of Corruption (1964), Ministry of Home Affairs, New Delhi.

16. Johnston, M. (1997), 'What Can Be Done about Entrenched Corruption?', World Bank, Washington, D.C.

17. Das, S.K. (2001), *Public Office, Private Interest*, Oxford University Press, New Delhi.

18. Verma, J.S. (2004), 'Role of Law Enforcement Agencies under the Rule of Law', Kohli Memorial Lecture, 5 May 2004, cited in *The Indian Express*, 7 May 2004.

19. Report of the Arrears Committee (1990), headed by Justice V.S. Malimath, Supreme Court of India, 1990.

20. Pal, S. (1999), *The Law Relating to Public Service*, Eastern Law House, New Delhi.

21. Paul, S. (1997), 'Corruption: Who Will Bell the Cat', *Economic and Political Weekly*, 7 June 1997, quoted in Das, 2001.

22. Bhoothalingam S. (1993), *Reflections on An Era: Memoirs of a Civil Servant*, Affiliated East-West Press, New Delhi.

23. Dasgupta, A., Mookherjee, D. and Panta, D.P. (1992), 'Income Tax Enforcement in India: A Preliminary Analysis' (mimeo.), cited in D. Mookherjee, 2004, p.122.

24. *The Indian Express*, 20 May 2004.

FIVE

The Reform of Politics

In the earlier chapters of this book, we had considered some of the limitations of India's democracy, and the growing disjuncture between economics and politics in public life. In line with the vision of classical political theorists like John Stuart Mill and Alexis de Tocqueville, who viewed democracies as the embodiment of reason and advancement for all the people, at the time of independence Jawaharlal Nehru had echoed his conviction that 'the fate of India's toiling and downtrodden masses was inextricably tied to the country's democratic ethos and idea' (Nehru 1958).[1] However, as we have seen, India's democratic governance has not yet been able to eliminate the worst forms of poverty.

Despite some of its limitations, India remains the world's largest constitutional democracy, with a free press, independent judiciary, freedom of speech, freedom to join political parties, and free elections in which millions of voters cast their vote and choose their government. For the Indian people, unlike their counterparts in a large part of the developing world, these freedoms constitute a tremendous personal, societal and political gain which transcends all other shortcomings of the democratic process. An important task for the future is to further enhance the freedoms that we already have, and to remove some of the limitations of the political system so that a reformist and distributive economic agenda becomes a reality.

Over the years, there has been considerable introspection and discussion among constitutional experts, political leaders and the judicial elite about legal and other changes that are necessary to make India's democracy work better for the people. The report of the National Commission to Review the Working of the Constitution, submitted in March 2002, has made various recommendations to further advance the ideals, values and goals of India's democratic system. These recommendations cover a wide range of political, economic, social and legal issues, including Union–state relations and the working of Parliament and state legislatures. My purpose here is much more limited. It is to suggest only a few 'core' changes that are practical and pragmatic, and can help bridge the gap between economics and politics so that India can realize its full economic potential for the benefit of all its people.

Let me begin with a couple of proposed changes in India's parliamentary form of government, which have often figured in the public debate but which, in my view, need *not* be pursued. The first is the proposal to convert India's parliamentary form of government into a presidential one. It has been suggested by some experts, including a former prime minister, that the U.S.-style presidential form of government is more stable and would ensure continuity of the executive branch over the specified period. The presidential form of government would also provide one known centre of executive power, and enable the chief executive to form a cabinet consisting of qualified professional persons from outside rather than rely exclusively on elected members of Parliament. As a result, the executive branch is likely to be more competent, secure and confident in responding to the external and domestic challenges facing the nation. All this is certainly true in theory. However, the experience with the presidential form of government in several African and Latin American countries has left a great deal to be desired. Many of these countries have found themselves in deep and persistent economic crises because of the lack of checks and balances within the executive branch. In several cases, security of tenure had the perverse effect of making the chief executive non-responsive to emerging problems or not accountable to the electorate for executive actions. Even in a mature democracy like the United States, with over two centuries of experience of the presidential form of government, the current controversy over the decisions taken by the U.S. President in relation to Iraq illustrates the dangers inherent in vesting excessive executive authority in one person, however popular. In a developing country like India, with substantial economic power in the hands of the State, a presidential form of government could be more prone to creating a crisis of confidence. When circumstances are favourable and the economy is doing well, a single and progressive centre of executive authority can be an advantage in accelerating growth and initiating policies that may not be politically popular. However, during periods when the economy is facing an unexpected challenge or a crisis (for example, in the aftermath of the East Asian economic crisis of 1997), a single centre of executive authority may not be as effective. Similarly, it is likely that in a presidential form of government, the chief executive would be less sensitive to the need for a change in the policies initiated by him or her even if the actual results turn out of be negative.

On balance, taking into account both the advantages and the disadvantages of alternative forms of government, as they have operated in other countries, the parliamentary form of government seems vastly preferable in a diverse and multifaceted polity like India's. An important advantage of the present system is simply that it has been in place since the country became independent fifty-seven years ago. Despite all its shortcomings, slow deliberative processes, and ups and downs (including an Emergency), the system has proved to be resilient. Established conventions, judicial pronouncements and legislative practice, based on consensus, are also vital ingredients for the functioning of a democracy in a multi-party federal republic. India now has well-established parliamentary traditions and conventions, and the main priority should be to improve its working rather than changing the system itself.

Another suggestion that has often been made, to reduce political instability, is that of elections by 'proportional representation'. Currently, a candidate to Parliament or the state legislature can be declared elected if he has the highest number of votes, even if the votes polled by him fall well short of 50 per cent of the total votes cast. This happens because of the division of the remaining votes among a number of candidates. This is also true in the case of a political party which may command a majority in Parliament even with a minority of the total votes cast in an election. In the past two decades, this has generally been the case in India. In order to improve representation, and to better reflect the will of the people, it has been suggested that the number of seats that a party secures in an election in a particular state should be contingent on the percentage of votes secured by it in that state or constituency. There are several variants of the proportional representation system, including a transferable voting procedure whereby the second preference of a voter will also count if no candidate has a clear majority. In another variant, a minimum percentage of votes can be prescribed as a threshold for a party to get representation in Parliament or a legislature.

The proportional representation system certainly has the advantage of reflecting the will of the people better than the system of simple majority verdicts, or what is referred to as the 'first past the post' system. However, the proposed alternative is unduly complicated. It is also likely to be non-transparent for a large number of voters, more so when the levels of literacy and education among voters are very low. In practice, it may not reduce political instability if there are a large number of parties contesting the elections and local issues, rather than national issues, dominate voter preferences. Taking these aspects into account, on balance, in India it is better to continue with the established and known system of elections by a simple majority rather than experiment with a new system, which may not yield the benefits of stability and continuity that are envisaged. For elections to yield better and more reliable electoral verdicts, which truly represent the preferred interests of the ordinary public, the best course of action is to further improve literacy and awareness among the voters.

The Economic Role of the State

As argued in an earlier chapter, the main political problem in the making of economic policy in India is not the weakness of its political institutions or its form of government, but the wrong assumptions about the real political interests at the ground level. For as long as four decades of central planning after independence, the primary assumption of planners, economists and development advisers was that of a welfare-maximizing State, strenuously seeking to reconcile differences among the competing demands by various groups, and selflessly promoting the greatest good of the greatest number. Based on this assumption, it was assumed that the greater the intervention of the State (and its agent, the government of the day) in the economy, the greater would be the benefit to the people. Thus, it was assumed that if the government-owned banks allocated credit, prescribed the pattern of output by giving out industrial licences and determined the pattern of consumption, the scarce economic resources of the country could be used to produce goods and services at affordable prices for the common man.

Similarly, it was assumed that if the means of production were owned by the State and were under the control of its political leaders, the entire value added in production would flow to the people. Savings and investment would also be maximized, leading to the emergence of a virtuous circle of a large public sector, leading to higher public investment, which in turn would lead to higher growth with re-distributive justice. For the reasons mentioned in the previous chapters, the political motivations in the use of resources were, however, vastly different, inward-looking, narrow and self-centred. Instead of a virtuous circle, the expansion of economic power by self-centred agencies of the state, over time, trapped India in a vicious circle of low growth, higher poverty and periodic economic crises.

A priority for the future is to further reduce the political role of the government in the economy. The process of reform, initiated in the early 1980s and accelerated haltingly since then, needs to be firmly pursued. The political role of the government, in so far as the economy is concerned, should be to ensure a stable and competitive environment with a strong external sector and a transparent domestic financial system. Since the balance of payments position, unlike in the past, is now strong with low external debt, India must also adopt an aggressive 'open economy' policy with as low a level of protection as most competitive economies in the world. Open competition is the most effective deterrent to the emergence of monopolistic practices and monopoly rents. A reduction in the political role of the government and its ministers also implies a reduction in the ownership of commercial enterprises. The high-sounding term 'public sector' is really a misnomer in this connection.

The public sector does not really work for the public at large. The value added by the enterprises has been low, and instead of adding to public savings, they are now a major drain on the fiscal resources available to the government.

At the same time, the political role of the government in ensuring the availability of public goods (such as roads or water) and essential services (such as health and education) must expand substantially. A reduction in the role of the government in managing commercial enterprises and an expansion of its role in the supply of public services are two sides of the same coin. A reduction in public sector deficit and elimination of ministerial access to commercial activities will facilitate larger fiscal expenditure on public services and promote stronger ministerial responsibility for the implementation of anti-poverty and people-oriented programmes.

A related political imperative is the need for a joint agreement between leaders of major political parties and the trade unions of government employees to improve the services of the State to its people. Such an agreement to improve service to the people should be possible through a democratic process. Unfortunately, this has not been attempted and trade unions continue to press for more benefits for those who are already employed without a corresponding improvement in their duties to the public. Some public-spirited heads of municipal- and state-level government departments have made attempts to meet some of the most basic requirements of the people (such as birth certificates or the renewal of trade licences) without delay or corruption. However, even these efforts have not yielded results because of the non-cooperation of government employees. A recent example is the failure of the so-called Citizen Service Bureaus set up by the Municipal Corporation of Delhi (MCD). According to an investigative report, this is what some citizens had to say about the service being provided by the bureaus: 'I want my daughter's birth certificate, but every time I come, the officials ask me to get some new papers ... corruption cannot be checked even in a computerized office. I am being asked to pay extra money to get the work done faster ... The Bureaus were supposed to cut red tape, but more than a year later, they are anything but [sic] convenience'.[2] There cannot be a more severe indictment of the insensitivity of government organizations and their employees to the requirements of citizens. A political campaign, with the support of civil society organizations, is now necessary to make the unions and government leaders more responsive to the needs of their voters and to make public servants more accountable.

There is also a case for reducing the number of ministries and ministers in the governments. In 2004, some state governments have nearly a hundred ministers, and the central government has sixty-six ministers (the number would have been considerably larger if some of the parties that are supporting the present government from outside were also inside). Naturally, the larger the number of ministries and ministers, the greater the scope for interference, conflicts and duplication. A legislative amendment to restrict the size of ministries to 15 per cent of the members of the legislatures is welcome. But even this percentage is too high. However, since this amendment has been adopted only recently, with considerable opposition from some states, it is unlikely that the number of ministries and ministers can be reduced further any time soon. An alternative approach may be to keep the numbers of ministries as they are, but redefine their functions and responsibility.

A worthwhile principle to follow in streamlining the working of ministries may be to abolish all commercial and regulatory functions which are handled by other autonomous bodies (such as the Reserve Bank, the Securities and Exchange Board, the Telecom Commission, Electricity Commissions, the Public Sector Enterprises Board, and so on). In their place, ministries should assume the responsibility for monitoring the progress of programme implementation in physical quantitative terms in areas that are of interest to the public and where there is a need for the government to assume greater responsibility.

The 'rule-making' powers of the government under the Acts of Parliament, and the complexity of various legislative provisions and rules notified by the government also require a review. Many of the Acts, including Acts for the regulation of financial or economic contracts and the development of capital markets, are more than a hundred years old. These laws are anachronistic and out of line with the current realities of global trade, commerce and industry. What has made the situation worse is a plethora of rules notified by the government over several decades, many of which are not even accessible (but nevertheless remain in force). Cleaning up the legislative mess, abolishing outdated laws and simplifying the notified rules, particularly in the economic and financial areas, are essential. For this purpose, it may be desirable to set up a separate Standing Committee of Parliament, with sufficient powers and legal support, to complete this task within one year.

Over time, the 'rule-making' powers of the government, without any effective parliamentary oversight, have grown immensely. The main legislative sections of an Act may be precisely defined or formulated to indicate the purpose and coverage of various provisions. However, it has become the general practice to add an explanatory section or an omnibus clause which gives powers to the government to notify various rules to give effect to legislative provisions. These rule-making powers are very wide. The legislation often prescribes that the government has the power to prescribe rules 'notwithstanding any other provisions of the Act or any other laws in force'. These omnibus powers provide sufficient scope for the arbitrary exercise of powers (or vendettas against political opponents and particular classes of persons, including taxpayers). In some states, as political rivalries among parties have intensified, these rule-making powers have been used to defeat the original purpose of the Act itself.

An example of the misuse of a central legislation at the state level is the 'Prevention of Terrorism Act 2002', or POTA (which the new government has rightly withdrawn). The relevant sections of the Act (Chapter II, Sections 3[I][a] and 3[I][b] were careful to define a terrorist act precisely by identifying the means by which such an act could be perpetrated (that is, by using bombs, dynamite and other explosive substances). At the same time, an explanatory provision to these sections had the effect of conferring unlimited discretionary powers on the government to regard almost any action by a citizen as a terrorist activity. Thus, anyone who was believed to 'advocate, abet, or advise' or did any act 'preparatory' to a terrorist act could also be apprehended as a conspirator and sent to prison! Any citizen, however innocent, could thus be brought under the purview of such an omnibus provision if the government wished to do so. And this is precisely how the POTA provisions were used in some states by governments in power to harass political opponents. It must now be made mandatory for all legislative provisions to be precisely defined. The rule-making powers of the government under the various Acts should be abolished. There is no reason why all essential and relevant rules cannot be included in the legislation itself. If further amendments in the rules are necessary, these can also be brought before Parliament for adoption.

The Role of Small Parties

Another vital political imperative for the future is to reduce the role of small parties (with a small number of members in Parliament or legislatures) and their influence in determining a government's economic agenda. Some of these parties, with less than 5 per cent of the national votes and an even smaller number of members in Parliament, can command a disproportionate influence in the government at the centre and pursue their own sectarian agenda. As an eminent journalist observed after touring the states of Uttar Pradesh and Bihar prior to the 2004 elections, voters in the state seem to have completely lost their power to influence the behaviour of their leaders. What each of the prominent leaders leading their parties wanted was only twenty to twenty-five seats (in a Lok Sabha of 543 elected members) so that each of them could emerge as a kingmaker after the elections. Thus, according to him, 'people of these states (Uttar Pradesh and Bihar) have lost their national clout. The politicians can afford to take their votes for granted ... nobody has any idea for Uttar Pradesh or Bihar. Nobody even has a promise.'[3]

This is a dismal state of affairs, and if small party formations, which are unrepresentative of the national will, continue to enjoy their growing clout, the economic future of the country will certainly be in jeopardy. Each party in a coalition government, however small its numbers, has become a power unto itself without being responsible to the cabinet as a whole. This is completely contrary to what was envisaged in the Constitution, and deserves to be set right as early as possible.

An equally important problem that has affected political stability in the recent period is the formation of governments by parties with a relatively small number of members in Parliament. In most states, while a large number of parties contest elections, the government is generally formed by one party with a clear majority. Occasionally, there may also be a coalition government of two parties but, by and large, the government consists of members belonging to a single party. At the centre, however, the trend has been in the opposite direction, particularly in the past fifteen years. For the first forty-two years after independence, up to 1989, with the exception of a three-year period, 1977–1979, the Congress party was voted to power with varying majority and it formed the government. After 1989, the picture changed dramatically and governments have been formed by parties which did not have a clear majority by themselves. The majority support was provided by a number of pre-poll alliance parties (as in the case of the National Democratic Alliance [NDA] government from 1998 to 2004), or by post-alliance partners and supporters. During this period, there were as many as four governments that were formed by a combination of parties with relatively small representation in Parliament with the outside support of a major party. In one case, the party that formed the government had less than even 10 per cent of the representation in the Lok Sabha. The fate of these governments naturally depended on the continued support of one or more parties outside the government, and these governments had very little room for manoeuvre when deciding policies or giving direction to the economy.

The formation of governments by parties with a relatively small presence in Parliament or by parties with the inside and outside support of a number of small parties has been an important cause of political instability during the post-1989 period, and its adverse consequences for governance and administration. In view of the unsatisfactory experience of the functioning of unstable and short-term governments, it is now essential to make necessary legislative amendments to ensure that: (a) a government cannot be formed by a party and its pre-poll allies with, say, less than 40 per cent of the seats in Parliament with post-electoral inside or outside support of other parties; (b) a majority government cannot be permitted to take office with the outside support of a major party which has a *larger* number of members in the Lok Sabha than the party forming the government; and (c) no party which has less than 10 per cent of the members in the Lok Sabha (or, say, fifty members in a House of 543 members) can be a part of the government unless it drops its separate identity as a party at the centre and joins the leading party as an associate or an affiliate member until the next elections. In other words, very small parties which decide to be represented in the central cabinet should not have a separate identity in Parliament. Alternatively, if these small parties wish to maintain their separate identities, they can always choose to support the government from outside.

These proposals should help in reducing political instability and providing governments with greater authority to take appropriate executive decisions, particularly during periods of external or domestic economic crises or problems such as inflation or financial instability. If there is no clear or at least substantial electoral verdict in favour of a party to form a government, it would be much better to have fresh elections under a caretaker government rather than allow a new government to take office which has no clear mandate and which is not expected to last. Several of our past economic crises arose because of the inability of governments dependent on the outside support of major parties to take timely corrective decisions. This was true in 1979 and again in 1990.

Thus, as is well known, in 1979, India was badly affected by the oil crisis when the Janata Dal government, elected in 1977 after the Emergency, was in power. However, in July 1979, in view of internal dissensions, Prime Minister Morarji Desai had to resign and Charan Singh was sworn in as head of government with the support of the Congress party from outside. This government also had to give up office after a few months because of the withdrawal of Congress support. As a result of political instability, the economic crisis became deeper and more difficult to resolve. The same situation occurred again in mid-1990, after the Gulf war, when the future of the Janata Dal government, led by V.P. Singh, became highly uncertain. The party had to split in November 1990, and a new minority government led by Chandra Shekhar was formed—once again with the support of the Congress from outside. The new government was, however, not allowed to present the regular budget in February 1991, and India had to go through one of the worst economic crises in its post-independence history.

On the other hand, an important reason why economic crises could be effectively tackled in 1980 and 1991 was the emergence of more stable governments which lasted their full term of five years. The same was true in 1997, when India was adversely affected by the aftermath of the East Asian crisis. The instability in its external sector was effectively tackled by taking strong corrective measures, which at the time were unpopular and thought to be unconventional. After the Asian crisis, India emerged as a country with one of the strongest balance of payments in the developing world, and the country's external policies are now regarded as having been highly successful and innovative. This would not have been possible if the post-1997 political outlook was unstable. Economic policy decisions to combat an emerging problem or a crisis are always politically unpopular to begin with, as they affect one or more of the special interests or activities that benefit from the existing situation. In such situations, a stable government is a necessary, though by no means sufficient, condition that makes it possible to be able to take difficult decisions.

Elections to the Council of States

A reference was made to the growing trend of the concentration of powers in the hands of a small number of leaders and the lack of inner-party democracy among political parties, large and small. This trend is nowhere more evident than in the process of elections to the Rajya Sabha, the Council of States or the so-called Upper House of Parliament. A specific number of candidates are nominated by party leaders depending on the number of seats a party has in the state assembly. Members of the legislature who are supposed to elect members to the Rajya Sabha have no choice but to vote for the candidates nominated by their parties. A candidate may have charge sheets against him for the most heinous of crimes against women or particular sections of society, or may be a financial agent of a particular party, but the legislators are forced to elect him to Parliament. This has caused immense damage to the reputation of an august house of Parliament in the public mind. It has also encouraged sycophancy and reduced the quality of deliberations. Taking into account the interest of the leaders of all parties in maintaining and enhancing their own powers, a radical approach to improving the process of election to the Rajya Sabha (such as direct elections on the lines of the Senate of the United States) is not feasible. However, a few relatively simple changes can be made to improve the electoral process. These are:

• A person who has been 'chargesheeted' by an agency of the central government (but not yet convicted) should not be allowed to be sworn in as a member of the Rajya Sabha. (This provision may also be made in respect of the Lok Sabha, but here political resistance may be intense. Please see below.) If a party still insists on electing him, the swearing in of such a person to the House should await the final decision of the courts. As in other important cases, courts may be requested to decide the pending case on an urgent and priority basis.

• Each party should nominate twice the number of candidates (or more) for every seat in the Rajya Sabha to which it is otherwise entitled. This will at least provide legislators with some choice of candidates of their own parties during elections.

• Elections to the Rajya Sabha should be by secret ballot so that legislators can freely exercise their votes.

• The domicile requirement for election to the Rajya Sabha should be restored. Since the Rajya Sabha is supposed to function as the Council of States, legislators should know the persons they are electing and candidates should have first-hand knowledge of the problems of the state. The domicile requirement should not be viewed as a narrow technical or legal requirement, but as a political requirement for effective representation of a state in the Council of States.

These changes will improve the image and working of an important political institution without substantially diminishing the present powers of parties and their leaders. It is to be hoped that these changes will command the broad support of all parties and can be implemented in the national interest without too much delay.

It may be mentioned that legal luminary and member of Parliament F.S. Nariman has made a much more broad-ranging proposal in respect of persons with a criminal record. He has introduced a Bill in Parliament to amend the provisions of the Representation of the People Act which would disqualify a person, charged with serious crimes, from seeking an election to the Lok Sabha or the Rajya Sabha until he or she is discharged or acquitted by courts. The persons to be covered by his proposed amendment are those who are liable to imprisonment for a period of five years or more or with a death sentence under the relevant penal codes. The Law Commission had also made a similar recommendation some time ago, but no action has yet been taken by the government. Mr Nariman's proposed amendment deserves the full support of citizens as well as members of Parliament, irrespective of party affiliation. However, if the past is any guide, and in view of the presence of chargesheeted ministers in all parties, the proposed amendment is unlikely to be acceptable. The resistance for applying the disqualification provision to directly elected members of the Lok Sabha is likely to be made on the fictitious ground that 'we are a democracy, and if people decide to elect corrupt persons, the people's mandate must be respected'. Unfortunately, this oft-repeated excuse has found acceptance in the higher echelons of the government, and also parts of the media. Public opinion may persuade Parliament to adopt the proposed amendment; until then the modest proposal made above in respect of indirectly elected members of the Rajya Sabha may be effected.

The Reform of Parliamentary Procedure

In a preceding chapter, a reference was made to the shrinking role of Parliament in holding the government accountable for its performance. The quality of deliberations in India's Parliament is diminishing, disruptions have become common, and its proceedings have become largely perfunctory. The functioning of Parliament, the maintenance of order and adherence to the rules of procedure, are supposed to be under the effective control of the Speaker of the Lok Sabha or the Chairman of the Rajya Sabha. In actual practice, this is no longer the position. A few party leaders effectively determine whether the proceedings will continue as planned or whether these would be disrupted and the Houses adjourned for the day or even for the whole session. Individual members, other than a handful of leaders, have practically no role except to abide by the dictates of their leaders (otherwise they face the prospect of being expelled or of losing their party nominations at the next elections). There are some independent members (elected with the support of various parties) and presidential nominees in the Rajya Sabha, who are free to lodge their protests, but they are too few in number to make any difference to the final outcome.

The shrinking role of Parliament was eloquently demonstrated on 26 August 2004, when contrary to convention and well-established rules of procedure, Parliament decided to suspend the question hour, and pass the regular budget and the Finance Bill without any discussion or adequate cause (such as forthcoming elections) within a few minutes. This was the result of a backroom agreement between the leaders of parties in the government and the opposition, following several days of disruption of parliamentary work because of a dispute on a sensitive, but extraneous, matter. The Speaker or the Chairman had no alternative but to go along with the agreement among the leaders of the major parties. Following the passage of the budget by a voice vote, Parliament was prorogued one week in advance of the scheduled date.

The events of 26 August constitute a new low in the working of Parliament and its democratic institutions. The passage of the Finance Bill by the representatives of the people and the Council of States without discussion was contrary to the spirit and the design of the Constitution and well-established democratic conventions. It is necessary now to take immediate legislative measures to avoid a recurrence of similar situations. Unfortunately, even all-party agreements on a 'Code of Conduct' or 'Rules of Procedure' are no longer sufficient to check unruly behaviour by members or the breach of agreed procedures. In case of unruly behaviour or disruption of proceedings, it is now normal for the House to be adjourned successively for a few hours at a time until the end of the day. As for breach of procedures, as long as major parties agree behind the scenes to the proposed deviation, well-established procedures can also be formally dispensed with by a voice vote inside the House. Seeing the recent developments in parliamentary practice, suitable deterrent provisions should now be introduced by legislation (and, if necessary, by amending the Constitution) to prevent disruption of parliamentary work and suspension of rules of procedure for conduct of business.

In theory, the Speaker and the Chairman have the powers to expel a member from the House or suspend him. But these powers have seldom been exercised. A convention has developed whereby the House can be adjourned in the event of disruption by shouting by a few members. It may be specifically provided, by legislation, that either House of Parliament cannot be adjourned more than twice in a week unless the listed business, including carried over business from previous sessions, has been completed. If the members disrupt work during more than two occasions in a week, it should be incumbent on the Speaker/Chairman to continue with the session rather than adjourn it. In order to help them in the conduct of parliamentary business, the leaders of the two Houses and the leaders of the opposition may be required to nominate two persons as 'whips' from their respective parties who would be charged with the responsibility of ensuring that their members do not continue to disrupt the House beyond prescribed limits. If the whips are unable to exercise the necessary control over their members, they should have the authority to recommend expulsion of the unruly members from their parties. The party leaders should be expected to act on the recommendations of their whip. Alternatively, in case no penal action is taken by the parties concerned in respect of unruly members, it should be mandatory for the Speaker/Chairman to expel the persons nominated as whips from the House and request the leaders to appoint new persons in their places.

In case disruption of the House or breach of procedures is caused by members belonging to small parties (which are not parts of the government or the main party in opposition), the Speaker/Chairman should be required to suspend or expel the unruly members after issuing a due warning. This provision should also be codified rather than left to the discretion of the Speaker/Chairman. Unless the penal provisions are mandatory, it is difficult to take penal action against members of Parliament or legislators in view of the traditions of personal courtesy and apparent friendship among persons in public life in India.

Further, a legislative provision may be made to the effect that the established rules of procedure for conduct of business of the House cannot be suspended or amended after a session of Parliament has been formally convened, except in a national Emergency declared by the government with the approval of the President. In other words, ad hoc and sudden suspension of rules of business, as was done on 26 August to pass the budget, must be eschewed except in an Emergency. From time to time, there may be a good case for amending the rules of procedure or business to make them more efficient. However, this should be done after due deliberation rather than all of a sudden, without adequate notice to members.

A reference was made to an important initiative, taken a decade ago, to improve the functioning of Parliament. A number of Departmental Standing Committees were set up to consider in depth the demands for grants by the ministries objectively, and make appropriate recommendations to both

Houses of Parliament before passage of the Finance Bill. Many of these all-party committees have done excellent work over the years and have made valuable suggestions. However, very little action has actually been taken by the government to implement their recommendations even though most of these have been accepted 'in principle' or 'noted' for further consideration. With the increase in political instability at the centre, the position has become progressively worse as these committees are reconstituted at short intervals and the turnover of ministers is also high. The new committee and the new minister do not consider themselves responsible or answerable for action taken on the recommendation made by the previous committee. To ensure a more effective follow-up, it is desirable to hold the ministry (through its secretary) accountable for implementation of recommendations accepted by the ministry. This is along the lines of the procedure adopted by the judiciary for ensuring adherence to its decisions by the ministries of the government. If the new minister wishes to change the earlier decisions of the government, he or she should be required to get the approval of Parliament for these changes after cabinet approval. The implementation of recommendations made by an all-party Standing Committee and accepted by the government should not depend on the predilections of individual ministers who happen to be in charge of a ministry.

Such changes in parliamentary procedures should enable the two Houses of Parliament to discharge the functions assigned to them by the Constitution more effectively. The proposed amendments may, however, attract opposition by some party leaders as well as political commentators on the ground that they are designed to curb the discretion and powers of members of the country's 'sovereign' Parliament and the highest legislative authority. However, as discussed in earlier chapters, the so-called 'sovereignty' of Parliament is largely a myth in the day-to-day functioning of the two Houses. All the powers available to Parliament under the Constitution are, in effect, exercised by the few leaders of parties in government and outside. The actual role of members of Parliament in determining the direction of policies, and holding the government accountable for its performance, has shrunk considerably. It is better to recognize the reality as it exists, and take necessary measures to improve the situation on the ground, rather than remain under a grand illusion about the sovereignty of Parliament and the untouchability of its procedures.

An important priority area of political reform is to provide for State funding of parties for contesting elections to Parliament and legislatures. In view of a large number of parties of different sizes that contest elections, an equitable formula for the allocation of State funds among various parties is intrinsically difficult. Even so, it is possible to evolve a workable and reasonable method for allocation of funds which reflects the strength of different parties in legislatures and which substantially covers their legitimate electoral expenses. A feasible approach, without causing undue fiscal burden, to resolve this problem was suggested in the previous chapter. Immediate legislative action in this area is essential to reduce the moral legitimacy of widespread corruption to raise party funds for electoral purposes.

These are a few urgent issues on which action at the political level needs to be initiated without delay. There are many more areas identified by the National Commission (2002) to improve the working of the Constitution. The implementation of the commission's recommendations by the centre and states, after due consideration, will no doubt take a very long time. If experience is any guide, it is also not unlikely that, in view of the political differences among various parties, the report of the commission will only receive casual attention and will be shelved after some time.

Even the few suggestions made in this chapter are likely to meet with political resistance in some quarters. However, I believe that this is a minimum agenda that the government and Parliament should consider and adopt, and thereby strengthen the democratic politics of India.

References

1. Nehru, J.L. (1958), *Jawaharlal Nehru's Speeches, 1946–49*, Government of India, New Delhi, vol. 1.

2. *The Indian Express*, New Delhi, 14 June 2004.

3. Gupta, S. (2004), 'Seizure in the Heartland', *The Indian Express*, 1 May 2004, p.8.

Epilogue:
A Resurgent India

If I were to look over the whole world to find out the country most richly endowed with all the wealth, power, and beauty that nature can bestow—in some parts a very paradise on earth—I should point to India . . .

There are many bright dreams to be dreamt about India, and many bright deeds to be done in India, if only you will do them.

—*F. Max Müller, 1882*[*]

At the beginning of the twenty-first century, there is certainly a resurgence of hope and confidence in India's future. The Indian economy has shown rapid and steady growth, and its potential for even faster growth is strong. However, as discussed in the course of this book, there are many hurdles—mostly self-inflicted—in the way of realizing this high potential. Although India has changed, and it has substantial new opportunities, our policy vision is still clouded by the concerns of the past. While it is gratifying

---

[*]*India: What Can It Teach Us?*, pp.6, 31 (Penguin, New Delhi).

that democracy is now deeply embedded in India's political system, the distance between political imperatives and economic necessity has been growing. The role of several of the highest institutions of democracy has undergone a slow but perceptible change. Corruption at all levels has become widespread, and it is now a primary cause of public disenchantment with the functioning of India's political system and administrative bureaucracy.

As observed by Max Müller more than a century ago, there are indeed 'many bright dreams to be dreamt about India'. While some bright deeds have also been done, particularly in securing independence from colonial rule and establishing a vibrant democracy, it is perhaps fair to say that a lot still remains to be done, particularly in respect of eliminating poverty and deprivation. Taking into account the recent political developments and deterioration in India's governance structure, in a previous chapter I had expressed some scepticism on whether India had the necessary will to further realize its vast economic potential. In this concluding section, I propose to take a different course and ask the question: What can we do to revitalize the functioning of political institutions and the economy to enable India to realize its full economic potential and remove poverty by say, 2020?

Policy Choices: Some Basic Considerations

In seeking answers to this question, it is necessary to have a broad agreement on some basic parameters of desirable strategic and policy options for the future. There are good reasons for widespread public dissatisfaction with the working of several of India's democratic institutions. Notwithstanding its drawbacks, in my view, our parliamentary form of government, based on universal adult suffrage, is also capable of generating as high a rate of growth as, say, China, provided we have the necessary 'will'. Despite the prognostications of some economic soothsayers, research has established beyond doubt that there is no correlation between the form of government and the degree of success in accelerating growth or alleviating poverty. In fact, two of the most successful cases of spreading literacy and reducing poverty in the developing word, namely, Sri Lanka, and Kerala in India, are democratic. Similarly, there is an impressive list of countries which have authoritarian governments but where poverty and deprivation have deepened and growth rates have declined. The adoption of appropriate macroeconomic policies and effective implementation of anti-poverty programmes are entirely consistent with a parliamentary form of government. In the past, if some democratic governments have failed or not done as well as they should have in the economic field, it had more to do with the adoption of wrong macroeconomic policies or lack of accountability in administration rather than their form of government.

In considering future policy options, it is also necessary to distinguish between 'ends' and 'means'. Thus, political freedom, alleviation of poverty, universal literacy, equal economic opportunities, and so on are objectives or 'ends'. While these objectives are non-negotiable, specific policies or 'means' that are adopted to achieve them are matters of choice. Unfortunately in India, there is a strong tendency to take ideological positions, on both the right and the left of the political spectrum, on instrumental options or policies to achieve desired goals which command general acceptance. Thus, for example, there is no disagreement about the need to generate more jobs or provide adequate job security for workers. Whether the best instrument for achieving this objective is through the expansion of the public sector is, however, a legitimate subject for reasoned debate. Similarly, there can be no two views on the desirability of higher growth with a better distribution of income in a poor country like India. But there can be a legitimate difference of views on the correct degree of the trade-off between the two objectives in the short run, or the right mix of policies to achieve the agreed objectives. In India, most public controversies on economic issues generally fail to make this important distinction between ends and means.

For a better future, it is important to have a consensus on primary development objectives for, say, the next fifteen years (up to 2020), and then have a debate on the means of achieving them. If we don't like capital markets, competition, global integration or foreign investment, then let us review their impact on the objectives that we agree on and choose the right policy mix. Similarly, if we prefer public enterprises or wish to confine the delivery of services to the poor to government servants, let us examine their impact on the agreed objectives of generating more jobs and poverty alleviation and then justify these policies on those grounds.

In view of the slow pace of economic reforms in India, there is a feeling among some that economic reforms are feasible only in a crisis. This was the experience in 1991, when India experienced a severe external crisis and then launched a process of reforms. The process, however, slowed down considerably once the crisis was over (by 1993 or so). Based on India's experience, as well as that of several other developing countries which have gone through severe economic crises followed by strong reforms, it is often said that the next phase of reforms would be feasible only if India faced another domestic or external crisis. I do not agree with this view—for two reasons. One, a slower pace of reforms, based on consensus, is vastly preferable. It is also likely to be more durable in a democracy. Second, a severe economic or domestic crisis is highly damaging to the economy and the people. The Latin American economies, for example, which experienced severe crises, suffered a substantial and abrupt drop in their national income and employment. The adverse effects of these developments lasted for several years. The poor were the worst affected. While crisis-driven reforms may have rescued the economy in the short run, the long-term effects on growth and welfare were largely negative (compared with the counter-factual hypothesis of slow and steady reforms without a crisis).

Among development economists, there is a strong tendency to package a set of desirable economic reforms in a standard basket. One example of this is the so-called 'Washington Consensus' on development policy. This term was coined by John Williamson of the Institute of International Economics in the United States to represent a set of policies favoured by the World Bank and the International Monetary Fund to free domestic markets, exchange rates and external accounts from government control, and to impose tight controls on fiscal deficit. Yet, it is not at all clear whether any set of standard policies can serve the interests of all developing countries at different stages of development with widely different institutional and market structures. Thus, for example, the widely favoured policy of encouraging foreign direct investment may bring substantial benefits when domestic financial and product markets are competitive. In other situations, when markets are fragmented or monopolistic, and the regulatory framework is weak, foreign direct investment may be overly capital intensive. In such situations, multinationals may increase costs and generate negative value added which may mount over time.

The cost-benefit of economic policies is likely to depend

on the domestic and external conditions facing a country. The right choice of policies is, therefore, ultimately a matter of judgement of those responsible for taking the necessary decisions in a country context. It also needs to be recognized that the validity or otherwise of the chosen policy mix has to be judged on the basis of actual results on the ground and not in terms of any predetermined optimal model of growth or capital accumulation. If the chosen policies do not yield the expected results, they should be modified or reversed as early as possible rather than persisted with.

A well-known economist, Albert Hirschman, has observed that the blame for economic disasters in many developing countries did *not* lie in the use of policies considered by economists to be wrong but in the blind pursuit of policies considered by theorists to be right—of the structuralist variety in the 1960s and of the neoclassical persuasion in the 1980s.[1] The lesson for us in India, based on the experience of other developing countries as well as our own during the earlier decades of development planning, is that there is no 'pure' or perfect set of policies that can work for all time.

The real world is complex and the interrelationship between countries and the global economy is also changing, particularly during periods when there are significant developments in technology (for example, the Information Technology or IT revolution) or political alignments (for example, the formation of the European Economic Community or the demise of the Soviet Union). The mix of policies that are required to adjust to the changing situation cannot fit neatly into any fixed paradigm. Today's global economic and geopolitical environment is vastly different from the situation that faced India in the 1960s or the 1970s. Our policy choices, and political rhetoric, must also change with the times if India is to move forward at a faster pace than was the case earlier.

I have referred to the power of 'distributional coalitions' or special interests in determining strategic or policy choices in India and other democracies. It has to be recognized that different sections of the people in all societies have different interests, and there is nothing wrong in this. In fact, more than two centuries ago, Adam Smith had attributed the success of market economies and neoclassical economics to the pursuit of 'enlightened self-interest' by market participants. In modern economies, workers have their legitimate interests in job security and higher wages, just as entrepreneurs and companies have their interests in maximizing profits and market shares. Consumers have interests in adequate supply and low prices, just as retailers and traders have interests in strong demand and higher margins. Similarly, farmers have interests in higher food prices, and governments have interests in ensuring food security at reasonable prices.

The real issue from a policy point of view is not that there are such special interests, but how these interests are reconciled with the public interest. If the pursuit of special interests leads to the adoption of policies which minimize the public welfare or which lead to higher incomes for a particular section of the people at the expense of the economy in general, then those policies are clearly wrong and deserve to be abandoned. The need to reconcile the pursuit of legitimate private interests with the interests of the society or the people in general is the primary rationale for setting up supervisory or regulatory bodies, such as a central bank or a stock market regulator, in most economies.

To sum up, an important priority in the choice of appropriate strategies and policies in a democracy is that these decisions must be based on a reasonable consensus (not necessarily unanimity) across the political spectrum. In making the right choices, we must also make a distinction between objectives (or 'ends'), and instruments (or 'means') that need to be pursued in order to meet the agreed objectives. The merits or otherwise of specific policies must be determined and debated in terms of their impact in achieving the desired economic goals rather than preconceived ideological positions. Similarly, the appropriateness of a policy needs to be judged in relation to the actual results on the ground rather than in terms of any optimal theoretical model or a standard package of reforms. If the chosen policies turn out to be wrong, they must be modified or abandoned as early as possible even if they can be justified on grounds of preconceived notions of what is the right thing for a developing country to do. India's policies must be tested in the light of what they achieve for India. Finally, it has to be recognized that different sections of the people have legitimate economic interests which they should be free to pursue as per the law of the land. However, if there is a conflict between private or sectional interests and the wider public interest, then the latter must prevail.

Having taken note of these considerations, let me return to the question posed at the beginning: What should India do to achieve its full economic potential? I will confine myself to some overarching issues in the areas of politics, economics and governance which need urgent consideration. Certain specific suggestions in each of these areas were made in earlier parts of the book; my purpose here is to try and identify a broad and integrated agenda for action, based on consensus, which cuts across relevant issues in different sectors.

The Politics of Coalitions

Harold Wilson had famously observed that a week is a long time in politics. The future is even harder to tell. Nevertheless, in India, particularly with reference to the experience since 1989, there is a growing consensus across the political spectrum that the government at the centre will continue to be formed by a coalition of parties, large and small, during the foreseeable future. The Congress party, which was in power for nearly forty-five years during the first fifty years after independence, was in denial for some time. However, even the Congress has now accepted this reality, and its electoral strategy is also governed by the compulsions of coalition politics. A large number of state governments are still formed by a single party, but the trend towards coalition governments of different varieties is also evident at the state level (for example, in Andhra Pradesh and Karnataka recently, and in Maharashtra for the past several years).

Another recent development is the importance of the 'anti-incumbency' factor in determining electoral outcomes, and the relatively short duration of coalition governments at the centre. With the exception of the National Democratic Alliance (NDA) coalition at the centre, which was in power for a little over six years (from March 1998 to May 2004) and which won an important election after losing the vote of confidence in 1999, no other coalition government has so far been in power for very long. There is, of course, nothing wrong if the government, or the parties represented in it, change after elections. In fact, it may be regarded as a most welcome feature of India's democracy. However, it is also clear that the combination of coalition politics, anti-incumbency and expectations of short tenure has had several unintended consequences which, over the long run, may seriously affect economic policy making as well as effective governance of the country.

One such consequence, which is becoming increasingly evident, is the excessive politicization of the decision-making processes in government, including appointments in the civil services, autonomous bodies and public enterprises. Thus, any decision, however injurious to the long-term future of the country, can be justified on the grounds that it is a 'compulsion' of coalition politics. This reasoning can be advanced to support the continuation in office of ministers facing grave charges of corruption, transferring civil servants with a reputation for integrity, and appointing executive heads of public sector enterprises for extraneous reasons. Even the high constitutional office of the governor of a state is no longer immune from the compulsions of party politics after a change of government at the centre. The politicization of the governor's office has been evident for some time. Whenever a new coalition government comes to power it considers it fit to dismiss some governors appointed by the previous government before the completion of their term. As often happens in India, this practice, which was earlier considered exceptional, has now become routine and a constitutional precedent for similar action by each successive government.

In other specialized public institutions, including the permanent civil service, where appointments are made by the government in power, there is increasing evidence of political considerations coming into play in the decision-making process. When a coalition government changes, very soon a whisper campaign is started and reports, usually initiated by self-interested individuals, about the political affiliations of the high-level officials and executives appointed by the previous government begin appearing in the media. Many of the previous incumbents are thus likely to be shifted or forced to resign on political grounds.

The justice or injustice done to particular individuals is, however, not the primary issue here. The potential problem is systemic. The pernicious effects of increasing politicization in the process of appointments are beginning to be seen in the performance of civil servants and other high functionaries. There is an increasing tendency to play safe, to curry favour with the new ministers by taking a critical view of the decisions taken by previous ministers, and to start a rumour campaign against other contenders for higher appointments or other preferred posts. These developments are leading to the emergence of fissures and divisions within the permanent civil services and other public institutions.

So far as the formulation of macroeconomic policies is concerned, the central government continues to be all-powerful in initiating policies, modifying or reversing them. Although the political context has changed and the tenure of coalition governments is expected to be relatively short, the concept of long-term planning is in place. A Five Year Plan for a particular period may be launched by one government, but the mid-term review of the Plan and initiation of another Plan is likely to become the responsibility of another government. States continue to be heavily dependent on central grants for carrying out various schemes and programmes, including anti-poverty or rural development programmes. Decisions on allocations of annual plan grants and other central assistance are taken by the Planning Commission (whose composition changes with the change in government) and the relevant ministries. Since these are political bodies and their decisions are discretionary, it is likely that the flow of central plan assistance to different states from year to year would be determined by the party composition of the coalition government at the centre and the party or parties in power in different states. With every change of government at the centre or in the state, the implementation of various plan programmes in different states is also likely to be affected.

Another casualty of coalition governments, their dependence on small-party formations (with a very small number of seats in Parliament), and frequent elections is the erosion of the concept of collective responsibility of ministers. More often than not ministers belonging to different parties are able to take their own decisions, or at least announce them, without necessarily having to go to the cabinet or Parliament and without any public debate. With each change in the government or its composition, economic, financial, education and other policies can be modified or reversed, sometimes for good reasons and sometimes for bad ones. Thus, for example, in respect of the financial sector, one government may announce mergers of particular public sector banks (without a public debate) or the closure of one or more financial institutions. The succeeding government, after a short interval, is free to reverse these decisions without any explanation. Similarly, price controls or controls on interest rates may be removed by one minister, but they may be brought back by the next minister without public discussion or notice. Or vice versa. The consequences of instability in the decision-making processes in sensitive sectors such as finance and human development sectors can hardly be overemphasized. While the political reality of coalition governments at the centre and changes in their composition from time to time is widely recognized and accepted, unfortunately, their implications for policy formation are not yet as widely appreciated.

My objective in drawing attention to some of the implications of coalition politics is not meant to undermine or question the merits of the electoral process as it has evolved over the years or our parliamentary form of government. To reiterate, there is no better alternative for India, and we can be justly proud of our democracy and freedom as citizens. At the same time, I also believe that it is of the utmost importance for us to take cognizance of the emerging political realities and take necessary action to modify the scope of discretion available to governments as agents of a democratic state. So far India has been exceedingly fortunate in having persons of calibre, integrity and patriotism in the top leadership positions irrespective of the nature of the coalition to which they belong. However, it cannot be taken for granted that this situation will continue in the future. The 'criminalization of politics', which has been discussed time and again in Parliament and outside over the past few years, is already firmly in place. As is evident from developments in some of the states, the politics of power is also becoming an end in itself. There are no principles or vows that cannot be sacrificed by party leaders in some states at the altar of power. There are, of course, still some exceptions to the rule. In time, such exceptions may become rarer.

While the country still has the good fortune of having highly distinguished leaders at the helm, some lines need to be drawn to redefine the boundaries of power of the federal government at the centre. Immediate action needs to be taken on two fronts. First, more financial powers and responsibility for the implementation of programmes should be entrusted to the states. This is not because all states are likely to be more scrupulous or consistent in the exercise of their powers, but because greater transparency and competition among states would at least ensure that better-governed states have easier access to financial resources and the opportunity to implement programmes. Just as the Finance Commission is constitutionally empowered to decide on the division of tax resources between the centre and the states, a similar Federal Commission should be statutorily set up to decide on the devolution of all other forms of central assistance. The allocation of non-tax central assistance should be related exclusively to the implementation of approved anti-poverty and development programmes in physical terms, that is, the greater the success of a state in implementing a programme in relation to its target in quantitative terms, the higher should be the allocation of central funds to that state. Second, all appointments in autonomous institutions, regulatory bodies, public enterprises, banks, and financial, educational and cultural institutions in the public sector should be entrusted to specialized bodies with a fixed term (set up on the same lines as the Union Public Service Commission [UPSC]). These appointment boards should follow transparent procedures for recommending appointments to top positions. Their recommendations should be invariably accepted by the government (as is the case with UPSC recommendations for entry into civil services and other appointments under its purview). Similar procedures, at arm's length from the government, may be adopted for top appointments in the civil services.

Another area where immediate action is necessary is that of lowering the bar on political corruption. Certain suggestions to reduce the supply and demand of political corruption were made in a previous chapter. A top priority is to provide for State funding of political parties according to a transparent and reasonable formula. On the grounds of compulsions of coalition politics, the tolerance for political corruption at high levels of government, Parliament and legislatures has increased significantly in recent years. A lid has to be put on the tolerance levels of corruption, at least at the ministerial level. Persons who have been 'charge-sheeted' for corruption, fraud and similar criminal offences should not be permitted to take the oath of office and function as ministers until they are cleared by the courts. A special procedure may be set up to expedite such court hearings.

Imperial and feudal traditions are still reflected in the

perquisites and various other public adornments available to ministers of the government. These offices should be made less attractive in terms of public display of power, ostentation and the personal staff surrounding them. There is no reason why a minister in office cannot continue to function exactly as he or she was doing prior to becoming a minister (that is, as a member of Parliament or the legislature) with some additional secretarial assistance. With ministers coming into and going out of office with greater frequency, it would be best if the gap in terms of ostentation between being 'in' or 'out' were reduced. Such a levelling of status may reduce the unseemly scramble for ministerial berths by legislators.

Finally, it is necessary to impose some discipline among coalition partners about making public announcements of policy changes without adequate debate in Parliament or even without consideration by the cabinet. A convention has to be established for ministers to talk less about policy and do more for the public in terms of the implementation of approved programmes. In any case, all important policy changes should be made after a debate in Parliament with the approval of the cabinet, and the issue of a draft white paper for public comment. New governments are entitled to change macroeconomic and other policies initiated by a previous government, but not without adequate reason and debate. In the long-term interests of the country, policies should be determined on merits and not on the basis of ministerial whims or personal ideological preferences.

I am aware that these suggestions, which are relatively modest but which reduce ministerial discretion, may be considered too ambitious and impractical in the present situation. They may also not be acceptable to ministers, particularly from smaller parties, who enjoy the pomp and splendour of their office and have considerable discretion to make appointments and evolve policies or reverse them. However, I also believe that the test of leadership is really in being able to do what is considered necessary in the long-term interests of the country, even if what needs to be done hurts some special interests and goes against current opinion. Thus, in the early years after independence, there was considerable scepticism about India's ability to survive as a democracy. It was the vision of Jawaharlal Nehru and other political leaders, and the personal examples set by them, which made it possible. Similarly, in the 1980s, after years of slow growth and periodic crises, the then prime ministers were able to initiate a process of economic reforms which gave India some stability and revival of growth. Again, in the early 1990s, during one of the worst economic crises when prospects for India were regarded as hopeless, the government was able to launch a programme of action which proved to be highly successful. India's political leaders have a similar opportunity now to ensure that the politics of coalition, in the years to come, does not undermine the country's economic future.

What can the ordinary citizen do to enforce the responsibility of political leaders to reform the system? This is a difficult question as people, taken individually, have very little power or organizational support to express their views and choices, except at the time of elections. During elections also, choices are generally limited to party functionaries, nominated by their leaders to contest the elections. Even after taking these ground realities into account, the position is not entirely hopeless. India is fortunate in having a very large number of non-political and non-governmental organizations (NGOs) in all walks of life. India also has a free press, multiple student organizations, trade unions with different political and non-political affiliations, and community centres in almost all localities.

Unfortunately, however, the attitude of most public organizations, including industry associations and media, is highly adulatory towards politicians in power. This is again a hangover from the British days when political and civilian authority over citizens was supreme and deliberately enforced. This situation must change. Individuals belonging to all public and non-governmental organizations, particularly business and industry associations (which have substantial financial resources and also access to the media) should hold politicians, parties and government accountable for their performance as part of their agenda and work programme. Everyone has a stake in the country's economic future, and the sooner it is appreciated by the leading business and other organizations of the country, the greater the chance of success.

Another important area, where all citizens can play a role, is to ensure that the movement towards universal literacy is accelerated. There is already a strong countrywide consensus on this score. However, the progress in reaching this goal has been slower than planned. All local institutions, including panchayats, have to assume greater responsibility in this area. Literacy among all those who are entitled to vote and select their representatives in local bodies, legislatures and Parliament would ensure that political leaders are accountable for delivering what they promise to the people in their manifestos or their joint Common Minimum Programmes.

Fiscal Empowerment

Twenty-five years ago, Janos Kornai, the eminent Hungarian economist, introduced the concept of 'soft budget constraint' in the literature on economic management in socialist economies.[2] At that time, Hungary and some other erstwhile socialist economies were experiencing substantial fiscal bottlenecks in providing relief and social security to their people because of the drain of fiscal resources in financing the losses of public enterprises, meeting large salary bills for government employees, and invisible or visible price controls in areas where public enterprises were dominant suppliers. Although fiscal deficits were high, the government was, for all practical purposes, 'fiscally disempowered' to implement any development programme, maintain or expand infrastructure facilities, or provide efficient low-cost services to the public. Kornai's concept of the soft budget constraint is of seminal importance and captures the Indian reality surprisingly well. In explaining the reasons for the 'soft budget' syndrome, Kornai was of the view that such financial behaviour was generally associated with the paternalistic role of the state towards economic organizations, including private producers.

There are several different ways in which the paternalistic behaviour of the government could lead to the emergence of fiscal costs without corresponding benefits. Among these are:

Soft subsidies: These are non-merit subsidies which are negotiable, open-ended, and subject to bargaining and lobbying.

Soft taxation: This refers to a tax system in which tax rates are not uniform, and where there are a variety of exemptions for different sectors and different classes of persons, including the better-off sections of society.

Soft credit: The credit system, dominated by public sector banks, is soft if it is used to provide concessional credit and unreliable payments are tolerated. Firms with financial problems are helped with further credit without real hope of repayment of debt.

Soft administrative prices: This situation obtains when the prices of products produced or imported by public enterprises (such as petroleum products) are controlled, and losses are borne either by the enterprises or covered by the government.

It will be seen that India's fiscal system contains all of the above features and more, which undermine its viability. Interestingly, while a mixed economy like India continues to be 'soft', many of the older socialist economies, which were Kornai's points of reference, have undertaken massive fiscal reforms, including privatization of public enterprises, to get over the fiscal constraint.

Since the crisis of 1991, when as part of its agreement with the International Monetary Fund (IMF) India had committed itself to reducing its fiscal deficit, the problem of fiscal deficit has been regularly in the news. Every budget since then has committed itself to reducing the fiscal deficit, including the revenue deficit. While three or four budgets since then have succeeded in meeting this objective, by and large, the aggregate fiscal deficits of the centre and the states have continued to remain high. Success in reducing fiscal deficits has been elusive, even though there is a widespread political consensus (until lately) that India would do well to reduce its deficits. More recently, in the context of high foreign exchange reserves, it has been suggested by some experts that higher deficits for worthy causes (such as assured rural employment or infrastructure) are worthwhile as emerging inflationary pressures can be contained through the use of foreign exchange reserves. As the arguments for and against fiscal deficits are by now well known, I do not propose to go into them. My limited purpose here is to suggest that, irrespective of the level of the fiscal deficit that is considered desirable, it is of utmost importance that budgetary resources available to the government are not frittered away in doing things (such as those mentioned by

Kornai) that do not yield adequate benefits in terms of growth, poverty alleviation or provision of public services.

Today, the central government is certainly in a position to print money (by increasing its monetized borrowings from the Reserve Bank), but it is a moot question whether such a course would lead to higher investments or only higher unproductive revenue expenditure by way of subsidies, higher salary bills, and higher losses in loss-making public sector enterprises. The experience has been highly disconcerting on this score. The government has borrowed more from the market or the Reserve Bank of India and its deficits have increased, but its capital expenditure as a proportion of total expenditure has declined sharply. The experience of other developing countries, which have taken recourse to higher expenditure by creating deficits, has also been similar, if not worse. Thus, according to Dornbusch and Reynoso (1989), the Latin American experience shows that the 'scope for deficit finance as an engine of economic development is extremely limited and extraordinarily hazardous'. Carried too far, they warn, inflationary finance develops a dynamic of its own that can set back the development effort by a decade or more.[3]

The reason why, contrary to Keynesian prescriptions, higher and persistent fiscal deficits do not necessarily lead to higher output in developing countries, despite the availability of surplus labour and underutilized capacity, is a puzzle. The answer perhaps lies in the behavioural dynamics of decisions on budget expenditure and the influence of non-economic factors in determining them. The softer the budget constraint and the easier it is to finance expenditure through borrowings, the greater is the pressure likely to be from special interests for subsidies, higher salaries and unproductive expenditure. It also stands to reason that if higher investment and growth could be secured simply by printing money and monetizing deficits, then no poor country would have remained poor.

The financial position of state governments is now truly alarming. There is hardly a state, large or small, that is not experiencing a budgetary crisis. While many programmes have been launched, including in the infrastructure sectors (such as roads, ports and water supply), they remain underfinanced with large debt liabilities. In several large and populous states, as much as 90 per cent of the budget receipts are accounted for by salaries, interest and debt repayments and losses of public enterprises. Despite large annual borrowings, most states are now fiscally 'disempowered' to undertake even minimal essential investment or maintenance expenditure. In a private conversation, the chief minister of a state, who prefers to remain anonymous, said that his state was not even able to live from 'hand to mouth'. It was living from 'hand to hand': monthly arrears of salary, interest payments to banks and other current expenditure were so high that all budgetary receipts had to be passed down the expenditure chain even before they were fully credited in the accounts.

These fiscal realities can no longer be ignored if the governments at the centre and the states are to secure a better future for their citizens. The responsibility of the state to provide essential facilities, particularly in non-metropolitan areas, and to create the conditions for growth through investments in such areas as education, health, water supply and irrigation is paramount. Unless action is taken to put the country's fiscal house in order, no amount of macroeconomic reform by itself can be sustainable. If lakhs of primary schools run by government agencies, thousands of primary health centres set up by district authorities, and hundreds of central and state universities continue to underperform or decline, two or three hi-tech cities and one or two new business schools and technical institutes cannot make up for the gigantic loss of human resources. It is simply a question of relative proportions, and inextricable linkages between public good and private progress.

The concern about the need to improve government finances has figured in budget discussions in Parliament and outside for at least three decades (after the first oil crisis in 1973, when stringent expenditure control measures had to be introduced to release resources for oil imports). Numerous committees and commissions, including Finance Commissions, have made appropriate recommendations for improving budgetary receipts and reducing expenditure. Governments, both at the centre and states, have also taken several steps to improve the fiscal situation. But so far, the overall situation has not shown much improvement, and as mentioned earlier, in some respects it has become much worse. An important initiative taken by the government recently is the notification of the Fiscal Responsibility and Budget Management (FRBM) Act, 2003. Under the Act, annual, and lower, ceilings have to be announced by the government in respect of both fiscal and revenue deficits until the desired targets are reached. This is a commendable step.

It is, however, likely that the positive effects of the fiscal responsibility legislation in improving the government's ability to undertake higher expenditure in vital public areas will take some time, perhaps five to six years at the minimum. This is because, in the short run, the government's access to market borrowings and its revenue expenditure would need to be substantially reduced in order to meet lower annual targets of fiscal and revenue deficits. Part of the gap may be covered by revenue buoyancy due to tax reforms. However, the government's overall expenditure would have to grow at a much lower rate than before.

There is no easy way out of this dilemma in view of the excesses of the past. The only possible way out for the government in the next few years (until the positive effects of the Fiscal Responsibility Act are evident) is to sell its idle or loss-making assets and reduce its unproductive organizational expenditure. Political compulsions make the choice difficult. But this is the only choice. The government would do well to evolve a consensus on this score as early as possible by fully protecting the interests of employees in government and other parastatal organizations. The government should give an assurance that, while all its employees would have the option to avail themselves of a generous Voluntary Retirement Scheme (VRS), they could also continue as employees of the government if they wish, and draw their full salaries and other benefits. Those who opt for the second alternative would be treated as employees 'on leave awaiting fresh postings'. Even if full salaries are paid, the cash position of the government would still improve substantially because of receipts from asset sales and elimination of non-salary office expenditure. In several government enterprises, annual cash losses are in any case higher than salaries.

Substantial savings and reduction in public harassment and corruption are possible by reducing the large number of government organizations and 'attached' offices which no longer serve any useful purpose. It is invidious and unnecessary to individually list such organizations, but even a cursory look at the list of central or state government offices in the local telephone directory would provide sufficient evidence of the non-functionality of the vast superstructure of a large number of attached offices of government. They were set up years ago for promotional, information or productivity improvement work, but have now become moribund. Large savings are possible by reducing the size of this superstructure without adversely affecting the interests of the staff or those of the public.

Greater fiscal empowerment of the government is an essential priority for the future. The policy choices are no doubt difficult, but if legitimate interests are protected, it should be possible to reach a consensus on the means to achieve this objective.

Legal and Administrative Reforms

There are only a few areas in which there is as complete an agreement among all sections of the country, including political leaders, judges and civil servants, as on the urgent need for legal and administrative reforms. The consensus on this objective has been evident, in varying degrees, over the past four decades. In response to the felt need, several commissions have been set up; the periodical high-level conferences of presiding officers of state legislatures and the Houses of Parliament have put forward recommendations; former Chief Justices of the Supreme Court and high courts have made observations; the civil service organizations have passed resolutions; and experts and journalists have written extensively in the media. Nevertheless, by all accounts, the legal delays in delivering justice and administrative problems in delivering citizens' entitlements have continued to mount.

As a vast amount of literature is available and there is unanimity on the urgent need for reforms, only a few salient issues need to be highlighted at this point. First, as mentioned in earlier chapters, the economic costs of legal delays (for example, in enforcing contracts among businesses) and administrative hurdles (for example, in setting up industries) are truly enormous. Based on partial data and research findings on costs of corruption and delays, in India these costs could be as high as 2 per cent of the national income annually. If there were no legal and administrative delays, and corruption had been reduced substantially, then India's growth rate in the past two decades would have been closer to 8 per cent rather than 6 per cent. This would have brought India's economic progress quite close to that of China, and set the pattern for even higher growth rates in the future. This is an important point to bear in mind while seeking solutions to the legal and administrative problems. In case perfect solutions are not feasible, or hard to find, even a small forward step in these areas is eminently worthwhile.

Second, if there is sufficient will and cooperation among different branches, the legislature, judiciary and executive, it should be politically less difficult to evolve solutions to the problem of legal delays. This is because various interests, which are likely to be adversely affected by the reduction of legal delays, are widely dispersed and may not find it feasible to evolve a united opposition to measures for reform. A number of commissions, including Law Commissions, have already made a large number of recommendations for expediting the disposal of cases, and some of these have been implemented. However, the progress in reducing delays, particularly at the levels of the high courts and lower rungs of the judiciary, has been very slow.

An important part of the problem is the plethora of legislative provisions on all respects of national life, some of which are more than one hundred years old and internally contradictory. The vast legislative framework, as it has evolved over the past century or more, provides a fertile ground for continuous litigation by unscrupulous persons and organizations. This is an area where a special and time-bound Standing Committee of Parliament, set up for the purpose of reducing and simplifying legislative provisions in areas where the pressure of litigation is high, can make an important contribution.

An initiative the judiciary itself can take is to reduce the number of non-working days and the length of court vacations. The decision to increase the number of working days may be combined with the enforcement of strict limitations on the facility for multiple appeals, adjournments and frequent hearings at different levels of the judiciary. In the computerized age, there is also no practical reason why all judicial appointments cannot be made in advance rather than with substantial time lags as is the case now. The executive branch can take the primary initiative to lay down the appropriate rules for appointments and promotions in consultation with the judiciary. It would also be appropriate to delink judicial salaries from those of the civil services, and relate them to conditions prevailing in the legal profession. A workable and non-discretionary formula can be evolved by relating judges' salaries at various levels to that of the top ten or twenty lawyers practising in different courts.

Legal reforms to reduce delays should not present an insurmountable difficulty if there is an agreement among the different branches not only on the need for expediting judicial processes, but also on the urgency of doing so. Administrative reforms, on the other hand, are likely to face greater political opposition as special interests in this area are united, unionized and affiliated to various political parties. However, as mentioned above, if the legitimate interests of employees in government and parastatal organizations are protected, and the economic costs of continuing with the present system are recognized, it may be possible to evolve a political consensus to reduce administrative bottlenecks, if not eliminate them. Recently, Arun Shourie, a reputed economist and journalist with direct experience of the working of the administrative machinery as a former cabinet minister, has done a singular service by highlighting the inefficiency, inordinate delays and enormous paperwork in the decision-making processes of the government even in the most inconsequential of cases.[4]

Some specific suggestions for reducing delays and administrative hurdles, including the need to revamp the organizational superstructure and improving the morale of the civil services, have already been made in earlier parts of this book. Here, let me end with a couple of general points. The administrative arteries are now so clogged that nothing short of a bypass surgery would serve the purpose. Instead of trying to expedite the flow of papers and reduce blockages through circulars and exhortations, what is needed is to create an altogether new system of governmental approvals where only a few cases of public importance need to be referred to various ministries for clearance. The vast majority of cases should not require a case-by-case reference to the ministries, and should be permitted to go ahead on the basis of self-certification (or certification by independent auditors where necessary). Such a procedure would also significantly reduce the scope for bureaucratic and political corruption.

It may be noted that there were notable successes in some areas where an effort was made in the past to replace old and cumbersome administrative procedures. One such example was the procedural reforms introduced in the mid-1980s in the grant of pensions for government employees. Earlier, the system was so paper-ridden that it used to take a year or more before a retiree could claim his or her pension. After the revamp of the system, thanks to the initiative taken by the then minister, such delays were completely eliminated. Another recent example is that of reforms introduced in the approval system applicable to foreign exchange releases. Earlier, every such release had to be referred to the central bank of the country, through an authorized dealer, which in turn referred it to the government, where necessary. In addition to substantial delays and uncertainties, the procedures had given rise to a corruption industry centred on foreign exchange markets (including the emergence of a flourishing illegal *Hawala* market). In the past few years, the old system has been replaced by a rule-based system largely based on self-certification. The new system has resulted in substantial economic gains in the management of the country's foreign exchange resources.

These are only a couple of examples where the by-passing of the old system yielded noticeable benefits. There are similar examples of administrative reform in other areas, including the management of the water supply and public irrigation system in some districts. Such successful examples deserve to be replicated over the entire administrative spectrum. Along with citizens' right to information and decentralization, on which there is already a strong consensus, the adoption of best practices for delivery of services should result in substantial cost efficiencies and reduction in corruption. These in turn would significantly raise the country's rate of growth.

Contents of Globalization

In recent years, a great deal has been written about globalization, both on its merits and its discontents. The issue has also figured prominently in the debate on economic policy in India in the context of the 'opening' up of the economy to international trade (through the elimination of quantitative restrictions and lowering of tariffs on imports) and larger inflow of foreign investment in the post-1990 period. Internationally, as well as in India, the term 'globalization' has been used in a variety of ways and views about its merits or demerits have depended crucially on how it has been defined. In one sense, it merely represents a fact of life, that is, geographical distances between nations are no longer as important as they used to be in defining national identities or national advantages. The world has shrunk and no nation can remain in economic isolation from the rest of the world without hurting itself. A corollary of this view is that the integration of world markets is beneficial for all participating economies, just as a more competitive and larger domestic market is beneficial for a national economy.

In another, quite different sense, the word 'globalization' is used to represent a shift in domestic policies which, in some ill-defined way, makes the national interest subsidiary to interests of other countries or multinational corporations. It is feared that opening the country to international trade or international investment will integrate an economically weak country to the group of economically more powerful countries. The powerful can then take advantage of the weak to siphon off profits and incomes from the latter. In a more political sense, greater participation in world markets is believed to represent economic dependence on dominant world powers, which in turn is expected to lead to 'political dependence or social and cultural absorption'.[5] It has then been argued that an inevitable consequence of economic integration would be a clear loss of autonomy. This argument is part of a broader critique of market-based development, which is supposed to work only in favour of the middle- and upper-income groups. Such development, it has been suggested, leads to the marginalization of the weak and the poor.

In a widely quoted book, Nobel laureate Joseph Stiglitz has given a new twist to the argument about the impact of globalization on developing countries. In principle, he has expressed himself in favour of globalization, that is, the removal of barriers to free trade and closer integration of national economies as it 'can be a force for the good' and 'it has the potential to enrich everyone in the world, particularly the poor'.[6] However, its actual effects on several developing economies have been extremely adverse because of the way it has been 'managed' by the International Monetary Fund (IMF) as a part of its conditionalities for assistance to developing countries. Part of the blame for mismanagement also lies on the United States and other industrial countries, which have a preponderant voice in international economic affairs but which are biased against developing economies.

Another distinguished economist, Jagdish Bhagwati, has suggested that, in order to appreciate the benefits of globalization, it is important to differentiate between 'economic globalization', which has a positive impact on all economies irrespective of their level of development, and other forms of globalization which can have good or bad effects, depending on their contents.[7] He is in favour of careful management of transition from a relatively closed economy to an open economy at 'optimal' and not maximum speed. Bhagwati has also suggested that there are some parts of policies for economic globalization (such as capital account convertibility) on which developing countries should proceed very cautiously. With some variations, Martin Wolf (2004) shares the positive views expressed by Bhagwati on the benefits of economic globalization.[8]

Against this background, in considering the costs and benefits of globalization in the Indian context, a few points should be kept firmly in view. First, the cost-benefits are entirely a function of what kind of globalization we are talking about. In fact, in considering the merits or otherwise of a closer integration of the Indian economy with the global economy, I am in favour of avoiding the use of the word 'globalization' altogether. It is much more rational to specify the precise content of the policies that are under consideration, for example, import liberalization, financial liberalization, capital account convertibility, removal of restrictions on foreign direct investment, and so on. In the absence of such specification, it is possible to put forward widely different positions on the subject of globalization in general terms with seemingly equal justification. Second, specific policies in respect of trade, investment, or capital markets, in order to bring about closer integration of national economies have to be carefully 'managed' by the country concerned in its own interest. It is very well to talk about a 'global economy', but all national economies or regional economic formations pursue different policies in order to maximize their own benefits. Thus, for example, industrial countries are in favour of freer trade in industrial goods, but not necessarily in agriculture or services. Similarly, economies with a dominant and large financial or banking sector may favour external financial liberalization, but not necessarily in their domestic capital markets. India should also adopt policies which maximize the national advantage (including that of countries which are similarly situated) in an international framework. This aspect should be kept in view particularly during global negotiations in the World Trade Organisation (WTO) or the international financial institutions (such as the World Bank and the IMF).

Third, in considering the possible adverse effects of greater openness in trade or investment, it is important to bear in mind that, despite some positive movement in these areas in the 1990s, India is today one of the most insulated among the large economies of the world. It is nowhere near integrating with the world, or being 'absorbed' by foreign powers. By any measure, China, a communist country with an independent foreign policy, is more integrated with the world economy than India is or is likely to be in the foreseeable future. India's share of world trade, which is a measure of participation in world markets, is well below 1 per cent. China's participation in world trade is six times as large. Annual foreign direct investment in China by overseas companies is one hundred times larger than their investment in India. China no doubt has its economic and political problems, but a loss of 'autonomy' or an 'erosion in the authority of the State' due to participation in foreign trade and foreign investment is certainly not among them. Since all major developing countries are aggressively pursuing policies to increase their share of world trade and foreign direct investment, India's *relative* share is unlikely to reach anywhere near China's present share for quite some time.

India's policies in respect of the global economy should be framed in the light of the above considerations. While there is certainly a good reason to be cautious about 'across-the-board' financial and capital account liberalization, the fears of economic dependence due to trade and foreign investment are simply irrelevant in today's conditions. In respect of capital account also, substantial forward movement is now feasible in view of India's strong balance of payments position and a competitive domestic environment. The possibility of external pressures, resulting in damage to national prosperity, is likely to become more real in stagnant and closed economies than in economies that are expanding by exploiting new opportunities in trade and technology. This is vividly illustrated by India's own varied experience in the past and the present, and is likely to hold true in the future also.

A Final Word: India's Tryst With Destiny

I have tried to identify only a few strategic and instrumental issues in the areas of politics, economics and governance which are overlapping, but crucial, for India's development. I am conscious, of course, about the uncertainties of making predictions about the future based on current information. As Paul Kennedy says in his celebrated book, *Preparing for the Twenty-first Century*, 'it is impossible to say with certainty whether global trends will lead to terrible disasters or be diverted by astonishing advances in human adaption.' Yet it may still be possible, he adds, for intelligent men and women to lead their societies through the complex task of preparing for the century ahead.[9]

As we look to India's future, it is possible to be daunted by the complex set of problems that adversely affect its progress. On the other hand, as we reflect on what we have been able to achieve through a participatory, open and democratic society, despite many limitations, there are sufficient reasons to be cheerful and confident. In recent years, the global environment has also changed in India's favour. There are very few developing countries that are as well placed as India to take advantage of the phenomenal changes that have occurred in technology, international trade, capital movement, and sources of comparative advantage of nations. As never before, India's destiny is now truly in our hands.

Which way lies the future? It is difficult to be sure. However, there is no doubt whatsoever that if the men and women of India have the determination to realize the country's vast potential, India's economy can become one of the strongest in the world in the not-too-distant future. Widespread poverty, illiteracy and disease would then largely disappear and democracy would have given the people their just rewards. Whether we have the necessary 'will' is the real question.

References

1. Hirschman, A.O. (1987), 'The Political Economy of Latin American Development: Seven Exercises in Retrospection', in the *Latin American Research Review*, vol. 22, 1987.

2. Kornai, J. (1980), *Economics of Shortage*, North-Holland, Amsterdam.

3. Dornbusch, R. and Reynoso, A. (1989), 'Financial Factors in Economic Development', *American Economic Review*, vol. 79, No.2.

4. Shourie, A. (2004), *Governance and the Sclerosis That Has Set In*, ASA Publications–Rupa & Co., New Delhi.

5. Kothari, R. (1995), 'Under Globalisation: Will Nation State Hold', *Economic and Political Weekly*, 1 July 1995.

6. Stiglitz, J. (2002), *Globalization and Its Discontents*, Allen Lane, London, p.ix.

7. Bhagwati, J. (2004), *In Defense of Globalization*, Oxford University Press, New York.

8. Wolf, M. (2004), *Why Globalization Works*, Yale University Press, New Haven.

9. Kennedy, P. (1993), *Preparing for the Twenty-first Century*, Random House, New York, p.349

Index

DATE DUE